THE FURTHER ADVENTURES OF HEDDA GABLER

BY JEFF WHITTY

★

★

DRAMATISTS
PLAY SERVICE
INC.

THE FURTHER ADVENTURES OF HEDDA GABLER
Copyright © 2008, Jeff Whitty

All Rights Reserved

AUTHOR'S NOTE

The lyrics from *Sally's Merrie Mistake* on page 9 may be sung to any period-appropriate tune.

THE FURTHER ADVENTURES OF HEDDA GABLER was commissioned and produced by South Coast Repertory in Costa Mesa, California, opening on January 16, 2006. It was directed by Bill Rauch; the set design was by Christopher Acebo; the costume design was by Shigeru Yaji; the lighting design was by Geoff Korf; the composer and sound designer was Paul James Prendergast; the choreography was by Art Manke; and the assistant director was Brian J. Sivesind. The cast was as follows:

HEDDA GABLER .... Susannah Schulman
GEORGE TESMAN .... Christopher Liam Moore
Their SERVANT .... Kimberly Scott
Their NEIGHBOR and OTHERS .... Kate A. Mulligan
WOMAN IN PINK and OTHERS .... Bahni Turpin
PATRICK and OTHERS .... Dan Butler
STEVEN and OTHERS .... Patrick Kerr
EILERT LOVBORG and OTHERS .... Preston Maybank

THE FURTHER ADVENTURES OF HEDDA GABLER was subsequently produced by the Oregon Shakespeare Festival at the Angus Bowmer Stage, in Ashland, Oregon, opening on April 19, 2008. It was directed by Bill Rauch; the set design was by Christopher Acebo; the costume design was by Shigeru Yaji; the lighting design was by Geoff Korf; the composer and sound designer was Paul James Prendergast; the choreography was by Art Manke; and the assistant director was Gisela Cardenas. The cast was as follows:

HEDDA GABLER .... Robin Goodrin Nordli
GEORGE TESMAN .... Christopher DuVal
Their SERVANT .... Kimberly Scott
Their NEIGHBOR and OTHERS .... Kate A. Mulligan
WOMAN IN PINK and OTHERS .... Gwendolyn Mulamba
PATRICK and OTHERS .... Anthony Heald
STEVEN and OTHERS .... Jonathan Haugen
EILERT LOVBORG and OTHERS .... Gregory Linington

THE FURTHER ADVENTURES OF HEDDA GABLER

ACT ONE

Scene 1

Darkness.

FEMALE VOICE. I feel tired tonight.

MALE VOICE. Mmm.

FEMALE VOICE. I'm going to lie down in there for a bit. On the sofa.

MALE VOICE. Yes, Hedda, why don't you do that? *(Beat. Suddenly, wild music plays on a piano.)* Darling! *(No response.)* Darling! Don't play that tonight! Not this of all nights! *(No response.)* Oh please, think of Aunt Rina! And poor Eilert! *(The music stops.)*

FEMALE VOICE. Of course! And think of Aunt Julie — and why not everyone else? I'm thinking about the whole lot of you, Tesman. I promise to shut up.

MALE VOICE. Oh, Mrs. Elvsted, how thoughtless to work this way while Hedda's grieving so. *(Lowering his voice.)* Why don't you take Aunt Julie's empty room? And I can drop by at night and we can work without disturbing a soul —

FEMALE VOICE. I hear you! I hear everything you're saying, Tesman! But what about me? What am I supposed to do at home all alone?

MALE VOICE. Well — the Judge will peek in every now and

then, won't you Judge?

SECOND MALE VOICE. With happiness. Every night. We'll get along just dandily.

FEMALE VOICE. Do you think so, Judge? Really? Now that you're the big shot? *(A loud gunshot, followed by silence.)*

MALE VOICE. That Hedda and her pistols! Darling, really — *(We hear a curtain pull back. He screams, agonizingly.)* She shot herself! She shot herself in the head! Oh God, just imagine, oh … *(He sobs.)*

SECOND MALE VOICE. My God. People don't do things like that. *(Lights up. Hedda Gabler sprawls on an empty stage on a blood-spattered sofa. She's a beautiful woman of thirty. She clutches a pistol in her hand. She looks quite dead. Tesman enters good-naturedly, with a book.)*

TESMAN. Good morning, darling! *(Hedda stirs. Tesman notices the bloodstain.)* Hedda? Oh, you didn't go off and shoot yourself again, did you?

HEDDA. *(Groggy.)* Did I miss? *(Tesman gingerly takes her weapon.)*

TESMAN. Now where on earth did you find your gun? I always think I hid it for good, and then you find it again. Imagine that! *(He exits with the gun.)*

HEDDA. What?

TESMAN. *(Offstage.)* Oh, Hedda, I always pray you've killed yourself for the last time.

HEDDA. Where am I? Last night — was — Aunt Rina, she died, and Eilert, he shot himself, and —

TESMAN. *(Offstage.)* Darling, that was ages ago. We're far, far away from that place. *(He reenters.)* All that matters is that we're together.

HEDDA. Am I in Hell?

TESMAN. No, darling.

HEDDA. Where's the pistol?

TESMAN. You can look and look but you'll never find where I hid the pistol. Oh, what a mess this is! *(Shouting off.)* Mammy? Oh, Mammy!

MAMMY. *(Offstage.)* I's comin'. *(Mammy ambles in. She's a generously sized African-American slave. Tesman points at the bloodstain.)* Aww, Miss Hedda, whatchu doin' puttin dat dang gun to yo haid? And after I's gwynne get de room all good and cleaned up after de mess you's all makin'. *(She reaches in her apron and pulls out a plastic spray bottle of "Shout." She begins cleaning the bloodstain.)*

HEDDA. Who is that?

TESMAN. Hedda, this is Mammy.

MAMMY. *(Rolling her eyes.)* Hello, Miss Hedda. *(To Tesman:)* I tell you, if it ain't enough cleanin' up her dad-blame mess every time she decides to try comin' home to Jesus, I also gotta be all friendly like we don't know who each other is.

HEDDA. But I don't know who you are!

MAMMY. Oh, you do, Miss Hedda. And you don't like me, no not one bit. It always turn out de same after awhiles, once you get back up on yo' feet. Nowadays, when I sees you's all confused after you gwynne go shootin' yoself, I learns not to hold my tongue 'coz I gots ta get de advantage while I cain. 'Coz soon enough you find dat tongue a yours and hoo-whee we's in for a long sit!

HEDDA. Oh my God, what's happening?

TESMAN. Well Hedda, you're — you're in a special place, now. Oh, I'm never good at handling this. Mammy, do you mind running and getting —

MAMMY. Sho nuff, I go get her. *(She exits.)*

HEDDA. So.

TESMAN. Um. Hmn.

HEDDA. Who was that person in here just now?

TESMAN. Oh, her? She's our — employee.

HEDDA. Did she come with the circus?

TESMAN. No, no, she's a friend.

HEDDA. We don't have savages in Norway.

TESMAN. We're not in Norway. *(Mammy reenters.)*

MAMMY. Right this way, Missus. *(An energetic middle-aged woman bustles in, wearing an elaborate tunic. Mammy exits.)*

TESMAN. Here she is!

MEDEA. Good morning, George. Oh, Hedda, darling, really.

HEDDA. Who is she? *(To Medea.)* Who are you?

MEDEA. I'm your friend.

HEDDA. Why are you dressed like that? *(To Tesman.)* Who is she?

MEDEA. My name is Medea and I'm here to help you. *(Hedda begins to laugh.)* Is that amusing?

HEDDA. Who would name their child Medea?

MEDEA. My mother and father, I suppose.

HEDDA. But Medea killed her children.

MEDEA. *(Upset.)* Please, please don't bring up the children. Our relationship is very complicated. *(Recovering.)* But let's get down to business. *(To Tesman.)* Where did you hide the pistol?

TESMAN. (*Stage whisper.*) If I tell you where, Hedda will find it.

MEDEA. Tesman, you don't want me angry at you.

TESMAN. Oh goodness, no.

MEDEA. So where did you hide the pistol?

TESMAN. In the silverware drawer.

MEDEA. (*Terrifyingly.*) Oh Gods, why have you cursed me with such torment? Hide it better, Tesman.

TESMAN. Yes, Ma'am. (*He scurries off. Medea sits comfortingly next to Hedda.*)

MEDEA. Darling, we're hiding the gun for your own protection.

HEDDA. What in God's name is happening to me? (*Mammy enters, with tea and scones.*)

MEDEA. Oh, glorious. Thank you, Mammy. (*She takes a scone and a tea.*) Hedda, would you like sugar?

MAMMY. I's already put it in. Miss Hedda always take two.

HEDDA. How does she know that?

MEDEA. We've been together — all of us — for a long time, darling. When you shot yourself, your memory was erased all the way back to the end of your story. (*To Mammy.*) Very good, Mammy.

MAMMY. Yassum. (*Mammy exits.*)

HEDDA. I don't understand.

MEDEA. Tell me the last thing you remember before you woke up just now.

HEDDA. Tesman — he was in the sitting room with Mrs. Elvsted and the Judge, and I — played the piano, and then — I got an idea. And I took my father's gun and shot myself.

MEDEA. And that's the last thing you recall?

HEDDA. Of course! (*Searching Medea's face.*) What's happened since then?

MEDEA. We spend our days the best we can, here, waiting to be forgotten.

HEDDA. But what is "here"?

MEDEA. A world of infinite possibility coupled with heartrending limitations. For all of us here are fictions, Hedda, and in this place we must endure until at last we are forgot.

HEDDA. I'm not — a fiction! How ridiculous!

MEDEA. Utterly, yes, but also TRUE! And consider yourself lucky! We're survivors, you and me. Most of us here face a hasty death. Desperate characters wander the streets — hundreds of them — facing their last wretched minutes of existence. (*A young*

1920s flapper enters.) You — get out, you!

FLOSSIE. Oh, hi.

MEDEA. I know what you're up to, and we have no time to waste on your kind! Begone!

FLOSSIE. No — no, I need attention! Please! Look at me — I'm sassy and sexy and I set men's hearts aflutter! I can sing! I can dance! Look, look! *(She begins a frantic Charleston, and swoons.)* I'm fading! I feel it — *(Pointing at her heart.)* — right here! Oh my God! Please, please look at me! Aren't I memorable? Help me, anybody, help me!

MEDEA. *(To Hedda.)* Well, here we do have a case in point. From where do you hail, O loathsome chorine?

FLOSSIE. *Sally's Merrie Mistake of 1927.* A wonderful show, really! I'm Sally's sidekick Flossie and I'm bent on making it in show business and I do a big song and dance number for a Broadway producer — it's gangbusters! *(She sings:)*
> HEY MISTER MAN, OH WONTCHA BABY ME?
> I WILL BE YOUR BABY IF YOU'LL BE MY DADDY!
> HOLD A BOTTLE TO MY LIPS AND WATCH 'EM
> PUCKER
> LOOSEN UP MY HIPS 'COZ YOU'RE MY ALL-DAY
> SUCKER!

And then I kick like this and do a little — *(She falls down dead.)*

MEDEA. It's a fate that could befall any of us, one day.

HEDDA. Is she —

MEDEA. The last memory of giddy young Flossie is now forgot, and she is quite dead. Shocking at first, but you'll get used to it.

HEDDA. But how did I get here?

MEDEA. You emerged from the womb of us all, Hedda. *(Gravely.)* The Furnace.

HEDDA. What's that?

MEDEA. Ohhhh, my child. The Furnace is the place of our birth, where every fictional character is invented. It is the life-force, the fountain of creation. And after we are born from it, we must bear the brutal winds of history. It is a terrible sight to behold, for the countryside around The Furnace is piled high with the dead, those unfortunates who lingered only briefly before their legacy evaporated.

HEDDA. Evaporated?

MEDEA. They were badly written. Or well written, and unlucky.

HEDDA. But — I survived?

9

MEDEA. Yes! Because your creator was a GENIUS! As was mine! So we PERSIST! *(Frowning at the chorine's body.)* You can't keep anything nice around here. Mammy! *(Mammy enters.)*

MAMMY. Yassum? *(Medea points at the chorine.)* Oh Lawdy what a mornin'. I go stack her up wit de others. *(She goes to the body and begins dragging it offstage.)*

MEDEA. Of course, not everyone who survives can stand the test of time gracefully — Mammy, for example. She can't live with her own kind.

HEDDA. Why not?

MEDEA. They reject her, poor thing. Mammy is in her heart a slave, and for some reason that's not in vogue nowadays. She's a dear, dear creature and it's horrible that she's meant to serve people all the time. By the way, when you're done with that, Mammy, could you fix a wee picnic lunch that I can take with me?

MAMMY. Yassum.

MEDEA. You're a doll. *(Mammy smiles wanly and exits with the body.)*

HEDDA. But she couldn't possibly wish to be a slave.

MEDEA. And a beautiful young woman like you couldn't possibly wish to kill herself. But we are forever doomed to act on our natures, for good and ill, without escape. My little boys live in terror of me. They were playing so adorably this morning. And I cried out, "Darlings! Mommy's here!" and the LOOK that came over their faces! They were gone just as fast as their little legs would run.

HEDDA. So I can never change?

MEDEA. Unhappiness is your essence.

HEDDA. Then I'm trapped — in the exact situation I was trying to leave! What a morbid paradox!

MEDEA. Ah, yes.

HEDDA. STUCK with my horrible husband and his meddling aunt and — oh my God!

MEDEA. *(Holding Hedda close.)* Darling, I know it's hard. I'm a tragic figure myself, so I sympathize. Sometimes I want to treat you like you're my very own child. *(Hedda pulls away, a bit.)* You'll find it's not so bad, here. This neighborhood is quite lovely and exclusive. The Cul-De-Sac of the Tragic Women. We tend to stay with our own. *(We hear a long, operatic soprano trill. A body drops from the ceiling and lands behind the sofa.)*

HEDDA. Oh my God!

MEDEA. It's all right, dear. That sort of thing happens all the time around here. *(An arm pops over the sofa, and a bleary Italian woman pulls herself up.)*

TOSCA. Cara mia, where am I?

MEDEA. For God's sakes, Tosca, this is the second time today.

TOSCA. What happened? My lover, he deada, and I decide only way to solva my problem is to jump offa thata cleef.

MEDEA. *(To Tosca.)* Sweetie, let me take you home and pop you in a nice bubble bath. *(To Hedda.)* Can you tend to yourself, Hedda?

HEDDA. I suppose.

MEDEA. Please don't do anything rash. Give it a few days, darling. The suicides — of all of us in this world, you are the most difficult. But you must believe you will make your peace some day. Though you never will, you must believe you can. Otherwise your life will forever be unbearable. *(Medea takes a limping Tosca offstage. Hedda is alone. She rises, and clutches her fists in frustration. She rages around the stage, having a terrifying mini-tantrum. Tesman enters and watches her. Hedda sees him and jumps.)*

TESMAN. Darling, Aunt Julie's dropping by to have a snack and see what we've done with the place.

HEDDA. Oh God oh God oh God! Tesman, what am I going to do? I'm trapped here forever! Trapped with you, and your Aunt Julie, and — I can't stand it!

TESMAN. I want to make a home for us, Hedda.

HEDDA. I live! How on earth is it that I live?

TESMAN. Now darling —

HEDDA. There's nothing extraordinary about me! I'm a coward, Tesman. A coward. Why would anyone find me interesting?

TESMAN. I do.

HEDDA. Oh, Tesman, the gun the gun the gun! Where is it?

TESMAN. Darling, can't we share a life together?

HEDDA. No! Oh God, I must find a new situation! Where is your friend Eilert Lovborg? Is he here, too? *(Tesman nods.)* Then I will find him!

TESMAN. He'll drive you away. He always does.

HEDDA. But why?

TESMAN. You put his life's masterwork into the oven and burned it to a crisp. *(Beat.)*

HEDDA. And?

TESMAN. And you got him to start drinking again even though

11

he's a recovering alcoholic.

HEDDA. Mmm-hmm?

TESMAN. And you gave him one of your father's pistols with which to kill himself.

HEDDA. And he's still mad about all that?

TESMAN. I'm afraid so. We're trapped, Hedda. You'd think we'd find perspective here, but — *(He shrugs.)*

HEDDA. Trapped — again! Even here! Trapped by the cruel limitations of — of — that novelist?

TESMAN. Playwright.

HEDDA. I'm — a play?

TESMAN. Yes. I believe so. Play characters are much more talky and dramatic than those in books. They always have a reason to leave the room.

HEDDA. So all across Norway, people line up to see me, the daughter of General Gabler, parading around — the stage?

TESMAN. All around the WORLD, Hedda. For decades and decades. Production after production, in countless languages. Shooting yourself in Norway, in America, in England, in France! At THIS theater, BANG, and THAT theater, BANG — and always, the applause! The rapturous applause! For YOU! Giving you life — giving US life!

HEDDA. Oh God — my suffering, borne out again and again — for the delectation of the cognoscenti safe in their seats! One vain actress after another trying to fill my shoes, people applauding her for her courage — the courage to play such a wretched person as me! I would sooner die!

TESMAN. That's the problem. You sort of CAN'T. Oh my darling, instead of focusing on the negative all the time —

HEDDA. But isn't that what that horrible Hedda Gabler DOES? Gloomy mean ol' Hedda?

TESMAN. — Think of your endurance as a wonderful accomplishment! Look out there, Hedda — sometimes you can feel them, the people watching you, thinking about you, studying you, portraying you, writing dissertations about you. You live in their memories and their imaginations. They keep you alive.

HEDDA. WELL, MAKE THEM STOP! *(Turning to the back wall.)* QUIT PAYING ATTENTION TO ME!

TESMAN. *(Pointing front.)* It's a hunch, but I feel them over there.

HEDDA. Oh. *(She faces the audience, blindly.)* LEAVE ME

ALONE! Oh, Tesman, you're right — *(She squints into the house. The house lights rise a bit.)* THERE you are. ALL RIGHT, then. How would YOU like your lives paraded — invaded! — and dragged about for the delight of — of, say, THAT woman THERE! Look at her ENJOYING HERSELF AT MY EXPENSE! Well, I have a revelation for you, sister: It's all made up! None of my life really happened, so why do you CARE? Why do they all care? Why won't they just go away? *(She crumples, head in her hands. The house lights darken.)*

TESMAN. Oh, darling, for a moment I thought you were going to cry.

HEDDA. No one will ever get that pleasure.

TESMAN. *(Going to her.)* Darling —

HEDDA. Get away from me! *(She backs toward the audience, then turns with a scream, realizing they're behind her. She begins swinging her arms wildly, as though to bat everyone away.)* I am immortal! Oh my God! *(She storms offstage. Tesman chases after her, calling:)*

TESMAN. Hedda!

Scene 2

Mammy is washing a large pile of laundry on an old-fashioned scrubbing board. An African-American woman enters, dramatically, with a 1970s-era afro. She is sheathed in a remarkably long piece of pink, flowing fabric. She moves with a deliberate, sinuous poetry. She doesn't acknowledge Mammy's presence. She speaks to the audience.

WOMAN IN PINK.
    i. goddess. queen.
    cleopatra. nefertiti.
    jammin' down the Nile
    boat-men rowin' to the rhythm of my tongue whippin'
    snackin' and smackin'
    i doin the frug
    doin the watusi

mashed potato
i. queen. goddess.
i dignify everyone who see me.
and then the alarm ring
whippin' me outta bed with its lashing clanga-clanga.
and i, goddess, queen,
wash up.
not bein' listened to
by you
my man
indignified by
you / in the livingroom
tv on football on
you / not lettin' me into
you / rapist behind the eyes of
you / out with your friends all night
you / whippin' me with your words
sharp acid seed of
you / in my womb.

MAMMY. Well somebody get up on de wrong side of de bed dis'
mornin'.

WOMAN IN PINK. *(Turns to Mammy.)*
and between the now of me
and the cleopatra then
is a slave
a happy traitor
plucked from the homeland'n
servin de white folk
big toofy grinnin'
back-breakin'
shuckin' jivin' shame of our race.

MAMMY. Well somebody gotta get de work done. If de whiteys
left to dey own devices dey be sittin' like hogs in de mess dey make.

WOMAN IN PINK.
the color white wrecks me with its disregard
white innocence sting me like a switch
white, thoughtless like a ginsu knife —
and my heart: a tin can cut clean through.
white folk never save you, slave woman.

MAMMY. Oh, now don't be goin' on about de whiteys. I got a

fine view of what goin' on in deys head. Sho nuff. I knows who gots de upper hand.

WOMAN IN PINK.

you stewin in ignorance.

well, i sent here to save you.

all the way from 1976

i'm bringing poetry and politics.

mammy needs savin', we all say.

she gotta get herself out.

'cos you invented by whities,

a white lady dream you up,

and that's why they seem so comfy 'round you.

but now we gon' take you back.

MAMMY. Well, I's stayin' where I is.

WOMAN IN PINK.

you ever wonder where the mammys are?

you ever go out lookin' for a friend like you?

must get lonely bein' a mammy these days.

well, news flash, slave woman:

they don't make mammys no more.

you go to the furnace and see for yourself.

MAMMY. Den if dey ain't makin' Mammys, what dey's makin?

WOMAN IN PINK.

they's making PROGRESS

MAMMY. Runnin' 'round in dat pink tablecloth don' look like no progress to me.

WOMAN IN PINK.

you go on, check it out, mammy

you gon' see you just a relic

you gon' see you're an antique

not useful

not a friend

just an old zombie

best made

dead and right quick.

(The Woman in Pink exits. Mammy ponders a moment, then continues with the laundry. Hedda enters.)

MAMMY. Mornin', Miss Hedda. You have a fine sleep?

HEDDA. Have you ever wished you could die, Mammy?

MAMMY. No'm, cain't say I's ever be wishin' for dat. Life be a gift

15

from God, dat's what I say. Or a gift from whoever make me up. Dat lady who jus' left? She sayin' I's dreamed up by a whitey. *(Beat. Hedda's in a reverie.)* I ain't sho how I feel 'bout dat. Coz I's glad to be alive, but some days I wishin' for a relief from de white folks. But I afraid we's all stuck together for a long sit. Mm-hmm.

HEDDA. I wish I could die.

MAMMY. Miss Hedda, after some of de things you says to me I wish you could too. I offers to help you many a time.

HEDDA. Maybe if I found myself a new situation. I won't feel so trapped if I can move away from George and his meddlesome aunt —

MAMMY. If you leave Massa Tesman, den what kinna sitchyation dat be?

HEDDA. I don't know. Maybe — maybe I can find Eilert.

MAMMY. Oh, no, Miss Hedda, you gettin' in a pattern agin, like you SIMPLE. Lawd some days I wish you WAS simple, but you ain't anything near dat.

HEDDA. Where is he?

MAMMY. He done run off outta dis neighborhood, Miss Hedda. He don't wan' nuttin to do witchy'all.

HEDDA. But where to?

MAMMY. I hear he done run off to de Furnace.

HEDDA. The Furnace! Then I will go there!

MAMMY. But Miss Hedda, I's tellin' you, you bringin' yoself a world o' heartache.

HEDDA. But if I am ever to change, then Eilert can show me how.

MAMMY. Miss Hedda, it ain't worked so far. 'Coz you not be de changin' type.

HEDDA. So it's pointless? Pointless to hope?

MAMMY. I's 'fraid so, Miss Hedda.

HEDDA. *(Burying her head in Mammy's bosom.)* Oh, Mammy, Mammy, Mammy.

MAMMY. You sho in a reflectin' mood dis mawnin'.

HEDDA. Oh, to be REAL, Mammy! Imagine! Real people, they can say, "I'd like to change!" and they — they DO it! These vibrant, willful authors of themselves! They aren't trapped like us. They're FILLED with vigor and the courage to CHANGE!

MAMMY. How you know all dis?

HEDDA. Because — because I can feel how it is to be real. My feet are roots growing down to Hell itself, roots giving me WILL and

FORCE and POSSIBILITY. What if I were to say, with conviction, "I WILL be happy. I WILL find a way I can make myself HAPPY."

MAMMY. You never be happy, Miss Hedda.

HEDDA. I WILL BE HAPPY. See? When I say it, it's as though it were convincing.

MAMMY. Why Miss Hedda, today maybe you is changin'. 'Coz most days, by now you be bossin' me aroun' and lashin' out at yo poor Mammy. Usually by now you lookin' for de gun.

HEDDA. Really? Ohhhh, it's CHANGE, Mammy. CHANGE. I feel it. Happy. Happy. Yes. *(A moment.)* Oh, do you happen to know where it is, by any chance? The, you know ... *(Pulls an imaginary trigger at her temple.)* Not that I'm looking to, but it would save a little time in the future if I were to have a little downturn.

MAMMY. No'm.

HEDDA. Well, if later on you're, you know, dusting, or whatever it is you do when you're not — *(Gesturing toward the laundry.)* RELAXING, and you happen to run across it — *(Tesman enters.)*

TESMAN. Good morning, Hedda. Hi Mammy.

MAMMY. Mornin', Massa Tesman.

HEDDA. Hello, Tesman.

TESMAN. You seem chipper!

HEDDA. That is because, Tesman, I have decided that I am going to change.

TESMAN. What?

HEDDA. How long have I been going through the same old motions?

TESMAN. Well over a century, darling.

HEDDA. Then all of that behavior stops today!

TESMAN. Really, darling?

HEDDA. Really. *(To Mammy.)* CHANGE, Mammy.

MAMMY. Yassum.

TESMAN. What sort of change?

HEDDA. A fresh start. A fresh start for all of us.

TESMAN. Oh darling, yes, yes, a fresh start! So — this means you'll be kinder to Aunt Julie, for example?

HEDDA. Oh, this has nothing to do with HER.

TESMAN. What about — perhaps — being kinder to, say, me?

HEDDA. Meaning ...

TESMAN. Will you try, Hedda, to — love? Me?

HEDDA. Hahahahahahaha! Oh, George, absolutely not! To get

away from you — the whole lot of you, you and the Judge and Aunt Julie and the whole — whatsit — the whole CAST. That's my goal.

TESMAN. Oh. And where will you go?

HEDDA. I will go ADVENTURING. *(To Mammy.)* We can CHANGE, Mammy!

MAMMY. You sayin' I kin change, too, Miss Hedda?

HEDDA. The world is a new and glittering place for all of us!

MAMMY. *(Putting down the wash, rising, smiling.)* Well, glory be, den!

HEDDA. Now run inside and pack up all the stuff that you can carry. I need at least a week or two of clothes. Don't forget my green chemise. Several pairs of shoes. Aw, bring my entire trousseau just in case. And all the food inside the pantry and the books within the study. Oh, and my piano if there's room. Quick, quick like a bunny!

MAMMY. *(Her smile has faded.)* Sho nuff, Miss Hedda. *(She goes inside.)*

HEDDA. Well.

TESMAN. Oh, darling.

HEDDA. It was bound to happen sooner or later. CHANGE.

TESMAN. But — we may make decisions and it may feel like free will, but we always return to our natures in the end.

HEDDA. I will prove you wrong.

TESMAN. For your sake, I hope — oh Hedda, I'm going to miss you so.

HEDDA. Who can say?

TESMAN. You're set on this, are you?

HEDDA. Dead set.

TESMAN. Oh. Well, good. *(Beat.)* Darling, could you do me one last thing?

HEDDA. One.

TESMAN. Could you — could you reach into the end table and get what's in there for me.

HEDDA. What — what's in there?

TESMAN. My — Bible.

HEDDA. But you're standing closer to the end table than I am.

TESMAN. I just — I'm trying to get you to, you know, touch my Bible one last time. Just for good luck.

HEDDA. Touch your Bible?

TESMAN. For God's sakes, Hedda, open the drawer and take what's IN there OUT.

HEDDA. Okay, Mr. — *(She opens the drawer and gasps. She pulls out the pistol.)* My father's pistol!

TESMAN. Surprise! I thought you might want to take it with you.

HEDDA. *(Deeply touched.)* George, thank you — your generosity, really — gee, thank you.

TESMAN. I can't imagine my Hedda without her pistol! Look at it. Like it was designed for your hand. Feel it, Hedda. Its weight. Its heft. The worksmanship! Your sweet friend, warming to your touch … *(Hedda freezes.)* What?

HEDDA. You —

TESMAN. What, darling?

HEDDA. You want me to shoot myself.

TESMAN. No no, not!

HEDDA. You're trying to get me back to page one and forget everything I'm saying so you can — *(She waggles her fingers in a meddling motion.)* Well, you can forget it, buster!

TESMAN. But I don't exist without you! Nobody wants to see a play about ME!

HEDDA. *(Backing away from him.)* MAMMY! Mammy, HURRY! Get out here!

MAMMY. *(Offstage.)* I's comin' as fast as I cain!

TESMAN. Hedda —

HEDDA. *(Yelling off.)* Leave all of my junk behind if you must! You're coming with me!

MAMMY. *(Offstage.)* I is?

HEDDA. Yes! I can't be alone! We must get out of here! It's an emergency! *(She is staring, transfixed, at the gun in her hand.)*

TESMAN. But Hedda, you mustn't forget: we have our special secret.

HEDDA. What secret?

TESMAN. You know — the — the —

HEDDA. Huh?

TESMAN. *(Offering clues.)* You look so healthy … So plump and so healthy … Radiant …

HEDDA. What are you talking about?

TESMAN. The — There's an exciting development coming along.

HEDDA. Development?

TESMAN. A special someone in our future.

HEDDA. I have no idea what you're talking about.

MAMMY. *(Offstage.)* He's sayin' you's PREGNANT.

HEDDA. Agh!

TESMAN. Argh!

HEDDA. People don't SAY such things! Oh God, I completely FORGOT about that. When am I supposed to have it?

MAMMY. *(Emerging, burdened by several trunks.)* You been here over a hunnerd years an' you ain't had it yet. *(She stops.)* Miss Hedda! What you doin' wit dat gun?

HEDDA. George gave it to me.

MAMMY. Shame on you, Massa Tesman!

HEDDA. Come on, Mammy, we've got to RUN! Before we get SUCKED IN!

TESMAN. Hedda, I'm trying to save you!

HEDDA. RUN! RUN! *(As they're about to escape, they're suddenly blocked by a terrifying-looking Medea. Her hands and outfit are drenched in blood. Hedda and Mammy scream.)*

MEDEA. *(Feigning composure, hiding her hands.)* Oh — why, good afternoon! Feeling better, darling?

HEDDA. How could you?

MEDEA. What?

HEDDA. Do — what you just did — oh my God!

MEDEA. *(Pretending to be distracted.)* Do what? I was only — *(Cracking.)* OKAY. YES. YES, I DID IT AGAIN. And I feel rotten about it, I really do — but at the same time so POWERFUL! OHHH YE GODS! FEEL NOW MY WRATH! JASON'S PUN- ISHMENT FOREVER BE ENGRAVED IN THE LEDGERS OF THE GODS! *(A giant golden chariot, pulled by winged serpents, swoops down from the sky with a tremendous clamor. It stops.)* That's for me. *(She boards.)* Because I'm a tragedy, people assume that I died or committed suicide at the end of my play. But in truth, I cut up my boys and these winged serpents carried me aloft, IN TRIUMPH!

HEDDA. But what about your children?

MEDEA. Oh, they'll get over it. *(Yanking the bridle.)* HYAH! *(The chariot swoops off.)*

HEDDA. Even her. Even she cannot change. After all this time.

TESMAN. Darling, though we know that hope is futile, it's a comfort that it's there. *(Hedda looks at the gun for a long time. She throws it down.)*

HEDDA. Run, Mammy! Run like lightning!

MAMMY. I's goin', Miss Hedda!

HEDDA. Goodbye! Goodbye, old life! Goodbye, horrible house!

My renaissance begins TODAY!

TESMAN. Hedda, for God's sakes, be careful! Nobody knows what's out there! *(Hedda and Mammy are gone. Tesman sits, glumly. He takes the gun and examines it. He points it at himself. We hear a door slam, loudly, off. Tesman jumps and puts the gun on the table.)*

Scene 3

The world yawns open. Hedda and Mammy emerge in bright sunlight, traveling in a wasteland. In the distance we hear voices: a man screaming "STELLAAA!" and a voice singing "Maria ... " and familiar bits of dialogue echoing around them. People cross the stage in various states of dress — perhaps a Hamlet, a Cyrano, a Phantom of the Opera. Mammy and Hedda look about them, dazzled and confused. A female member of the nineteenth century Russian upper class enters.

MASHA. Moscow ... oh, how I long to go to Moscow ... *(She exits.)*

HEDDA. Oh, Mammy, I'm exhausted.

MAMMY. *(Laboring under the weight of the trunks.)* Sho nuff, you take a nice rest, Miss Hedda.

HEDDA. These people are so STRANGE.

MAMMY. Mebbe dey think you strange too, Miss Hedda. *(Jar-Jar Binks enters and sits next to Hedda, who notices him and screams. Mammy attacks him with her petticoats.)* Now you git off her, now! G'wan! Git! You should be ashamed of yosself! *(Jar-Jar runs off in terror.)*

HEDDA. Mammy, I can go no further.

MAMMY. Now Miss Hedda, you gotta be pushin' yosself, 'specially after de fuss you's makin back dere.

HEDDA. Carry me.

MAMMY. Naw, you's gwynne walkin' on yo' own two feet.

HEDDA. Perhaps it's not in my constitution to go further.

MAMMY. Well, you kin go back home but I's gwynne on to see what all de fuss about.

HEDDA. What fuss?

21

MAMMY. You not de only one lookin' for change, Miss Hedda.

HEDDA. But — Mammy, you CAN'T change! Whatever would I do without you?

MAMMY. Yo's own cookin' and cleanin', for one.

HEDDA. Oh my God!

MAMMY. 'N you be takin' dese trunks witchu if you go turnin' back 'coz I ain't coddlin' you no mo.

HEDDA. I can't carry all those! I'm sure the person who created me never meant me to do such things!

MAMMY. Well den. *(A moment.)*

HEDDA. *(Submitting.)* All RIGHT. Now which way do we go?

MAMMY. I dunno, Miss Hedda. Dere be lots of trails leadin' all whichaways.

HEDDA. Doesn't someone sell a MAP to this place? *(Diane, an African-American woman in business attire, passes by. She's on her cell phone.)*

DIANE. — Ferguson, I just got a call from the precinct. They found a juvenile female floating in a brook, surrounded by flower petals. Couldn't be more than sixteen. — Hello? Hello? I'm out of range. Hello? *(She passes from view.)*

MAMMY. Miss Hedda, you take a load off for awhiles. I be right back.

HEDDA. Where are you going?

MAMMY. I scout ahead and see which way de change is.

HEDDA. Don't run off.

MAMMY. Dat not in my nature, Miss Hedda. *(Exiting, muttering.)* Wish it was but it ain't. *(Mammy exits. A Grecian madwoman enters. Hedda spots her.)*

HEDDA. Excuse me, ma'am? *(Cassandra shakes her head, trying to avoid Hedda.)* My — friend — and I, we're looking for The Furnace. Could you point us there?

CASSANDRA. Speak not to me! I, Cassandra, most lustrous daughter of Priam, see naught but horror in thy stars!

HEDDA. You're Cassandra?

CASSANDRA. Aye.

HEDDA. The prophetess, Cassandra?

CASSANDRA. Aye, Lady, 'tis mine curse to prophesy forever true, but none beneath the vaulted skies will e'er believe my words!

HEDDA. So you always see the future, but nobody believes you?

CASSANDRA. 'Tis the curse of Apollo, aye!

HEDDA. *(Excitedly.)* Then let's make a deal. You tell me my future, and I won't believe you, but I'll follow your prophecy anyway because I have no choice because it's my future! Does that make sense?

CASSANDRA. O Lady, thou art kind to heed such a wretch as me!

HEDDA. So let's give it a whirl. Tell me: *(Taking her hands.)* Do I make it to The Furnace?

CASSANDRA. The Furnace, aye, a Hell of fire and death and torment.

HEDDA. Oh goody! How do I get there?

CASSANDRA. On thy sojourn thou shalt cross a rocky spate of metaphors. A darkened forest, and a verdant glade, and beyond that a lake most impossibly large. *(Suddenly, the curse takes Hedda, perhaps with a magical sound effect.)*

HEDDA. Wow.

CASSANDRA. Aye?

HEDDA. *(Amazed.)* That curse Apollo put on you is really some-thing! I don't believe a word you say! You are such a LIAR!

CASSANDRA. *(Turning to go.)* Thou art just like the rest, then.

HEDDA. No no no! Don't mind me, keep going! What happens next?

CASSANDRA. At the end of thy travels — O, misery!

HEDDA. What what what?

CASSANDRA. Thou shalt face a death most untimely and most permanent!

HEDDA. *(Clapping her hands.)* You're on a roll! Don't stop!

CASSANDRA. Reflect not such a troubling ardor on thine visage! For thou shalt bear a burden most contradictory — a crushing weight to make thine current sorrows as a teardrop in a vasty lake! A horror thou cannot this day imagine!

HEDDA. Oh Cassandra, you're totally full of it, but thank you! Thank you!

CASSANDRA. O lady, thine kindness maketh my day. *(They grasp hands and jump up and down, grinning.)*

HEDDA. Anything else?

CASSANDRA. O letteth me see — *(A vision:)* A boy with feathered wings of melted wax shall plummet from the sky. *(A moment.)*

HEDDA. Why don't we stop while we're ahead?

CASSANDRA. Aye, yes. *(She runs off. The scene shifts. Mammy is standing behind Diane, who's still on her cell phone.)*

DIANE. This is Detective Johnson. What's the skinny? —

Murdered? Two juveniles? But how? — Secure a locate on the parents. — What do you mean you can't reach the mother? — They're winged serpents. They have to land sometime. *(She snaps her phone off. Mammy approaches, shyly.)*

MAMMY. Excuse me.

DIANE. Ooh — you frightened me! *(She surveys Mammy.)* Oh my God, girl, look at you.

MAMMY. Yassum? *(Diane begins to laugh.)*

DIANE. Well if it isn't the famous Mammy!

MAMMY. Yassum, I is.

DIANE. Oh Lord, look at you with your kerchief on! Look at those HANDS — all rough and leathery from scrubbing floors, I bet!

MAMMY. Yassum, I works very hard. *(A friendly middle-aged woman appears suddenly. She's holding a bottle of lotion.)*

LOTION LADY. Rough, leathery skin got you down? Try just a dab of this! Put it in the heart of your hand. *(She squirts a blob of lotion into Mammy's hands.)* Now rub it in. *(Confused, Mammy begins to rub lotion into her hands.)* You can feel our patented combination of emollients and aloe extracts go right to work, soothing the sensitive outer layers of your skin. While the deeper layers receive the healing moisture they need through a revolutionary process we call "Skintoxification."

MAMMY. Oooh, yassum, dat is nice.

LOTION LADY. Isn't that nice?

DIANE. Okay — that's enough. You can go, now.

LOTION LADY. But —

DIANE. Your thirty seconds are up. Go on, get out of here.

LOTION LADY. Jeez, I was just trying to help. *(As she backs away, she tries to gesture to Mammy that it's good for her neck, too.)*

DIANE. Go! *(The Lotion Lady scurries out.)* Sorry, I'm from television. Those advertising people are like mosquitoes!

MAMMY. I don' get many people bein' nice to me.

DIANE. Those people know their time is brief, so they'll be nice to ANYONE. *(She reaches out a hand.)* My name is Diane Johnson. I am a highly educated, well-to-do crime scene unit detective with a sassy tongue.

MAMMY. I's Mammy. I's a slave.

DIANE. We've come a long way, haven't we?

MAMMY. Who's we?

DIANE. Women of color.

MAMMY. I s'pose. Can I ask you a question?

DIANE. Mmm-hmm. *(Beat.)*

MAMMY. Is dere a place I kin go? Where's I fit in?

DIANE. Oh. Mammy. *(She starts laughing.)* I'm sorry, it's just so funny calling anyone that. A place you can go. There must be a cotton field somewhere!

MAMMY. I's a house slave. And I don' wanna be servin' de white folk no mo. But I cain't help it. I's always comin' back.

DIANE. You try *Roots?*

MAMMY. Yassum, I's tried de *Roots* but dey don' wan' nothin' to do wit me neider.

DIANE. Maybe you should try accepting where you are in history.

MAMMY. But acceptin' IS my lot in life! Dat be de way I was made! I SICK of acceptin' my lot in life! First I be acceptin' I's a slave, and 'coz I made by a whitey I be acceptin' dat my people don' wan' nuttin' to do wit me — but I cain't be acceptin' dat I never be changin'! I tired o lookin' at de future and seein' dese people who looks like me but who's as strange to me as if dey come from another planet! 'Coz if I can't be changin' I gwynne — I don' know what I's gwynne do but it ain't gwynne be fun for nobody!

DIANE. I know what "you's gwynne do," Mammy. "You's gwynne" go back to living in someone else's house. "You's gwynne" be second fiddle to people more important than you are. Ivory-skinned people who have desires and wants and get their dreams fulfilled. You'll remain a bookmark in history. To be honest, Mammy, I'm glad I'm lost out here, 'cause I'd be embarrassed to be seen with you. *(She exits. Mammy stands a moment, by herself. She dabs her eyes with her apron, and goes back to Hedda.)*

HEDDA. I am refreshed.

MAMMY. Oh, dat be a relief, Miss Hedda. Sho nuff.

HEDDA. And I got directions.

MAMMY. To wheres?

HEDDA. Where the CHANGE is, Mammy.

MAMMY. Den we best be pressin' on. *(A sign appears, with an arrow. It says, DARK FOREST.)*

HEDDA. A sign!

MAMMY. What it say?

HEDDA. It's pointing us toward the Dark Forest.

MAMMY. Oh Lawdy, we cain't be goin' in dere!

HEDDA. Cassandra said it's the next step in our journey. And then, beyond that lies The Furnace. And Eilert Lovborg will be there, with vine leaves in his hair!

MAMMY. Oh, Miss Hedda, you cain't be finding Massa Eilert. He ain't in de best o shape after what you did.

HEDDA. Eilert or no, Mammy, if we wish to change ourselves, we must confront the source.

MAMMY. It look real dark and frighted in dere, Miss Hedda. *(We hear a chainsaw, off.)*

HEDDA. Do you hear that?

MAMMY. Dat don' sound so good. *(Chainsaw Killer in a hockey mask enters. He's swinging the chainsaw over his head.)*

HEDDA. MAMMY. RUN!

MAMMY. OH LAWDY! What kinna world be dreamin' someone like dis up? *(Mammy and Hedda flee in the direction of the arrow, leaving the trunks behind. The Chainsaw Killer lopes after them, then stops by the trunks, inspecting them. Little Orphan Annie enters. She sees the Chainsaw Killer, and jumps.)*

ANNIE. Leapin' lizards, Mister, you skeered me! And you know what I do when I get skeered? *(She sings the opening bars of an inspirational song. The Chainsaw Killer fires up his chainsaw, and chases her shrieking offstage.)*

Scene 4

Inside the forest. Tesman creeps on, cautiously.

TESMAN. Hedda? Hedda, darling? *(Beat.)* Hedda, if you can hear me, come home! We all miss you there! Aunt Julie is terribly upset! Hedda? *(No sound.)* Hedda, I'm frightened! *(A moment.)* That won't help. She doesn't CARE. And now, here I am — miles from home — when for decades I've barely stepped beyond the mailbox! Imagine the terrors that lurk in the forbidding shade of this wilderness! For not all fictions are innocent and kind, as I am. If only they were! No, some are scoundrels — villainous misfits who dwell in a dark, seedy shadow world! *(Two men enter. They're dressed in turtlenecks and have long, forward-brushed hair. One, Patrick, is quite effeminate. The other man, Steven, is only slightly less effeminate. Patrick carries a large purse-like bag. Both carry cocktails. They see Tesman, who doesn't see them. He's far enough away that he can't hear them.)*

PATRICK. *(To Steven:)* Oh, regar-dez!

TESMAN. What barbaric outlaws dwell in this terrifying place? I must find courage! I must compose myself!

STEVEN. *(Smacking Patrick with a limp wrist.)* You'll throw yourself at anything in trousers.

PATRICK. Excuse me, you bitch, but I do not THROW my person at ANYONE. I ADVANCE, implacably, yes. One in my position need not THROW.

STEVEN. *(Re: Tesman.)* She's not MY type, anyway.

PATRICK. Mary, everyone knows YOU'RE into rough trade.

STEVEN. I like my men less feathery.

PATRICK. What, are we cruising an aviary?

STEVEN. I'm tired of that pansy stuff. Flaunting it in people's faces the way we do!

PATRICK. Speak for YOURSELF!

STEVEN. Excuse me? Every time you open YOUR mouth a FLOWER falls out! What happened to being a MAN? Screw your courage to the sticking place! That's the kind of man I want!

PATRICK. Ooh, I think SOMEONE'S been spending time with Lady Macbeth because he needs a domineering MOTHER FIGURE! *(Beat. Steven suddenly slaps Patrick, the culmination of an entire offstage evening we didn't see. Patrick overreacts, hysterically bursting into sobs, collapsing on the ground.)* WHY? OH GOD, WHY?

STEVEN. *(Holding him.)* It's okay, Patrick. I'm here for you.

PATRICK. *(Long drawn-out sobs.)* Why-hy-hy-hyyyyy ... *(Handing Steven his cocktail.)* Hold this. *(Continuing.)* — hy-hy-hy-hyyyyy ...

STEVEN. Nothing ever comes easy, does it?

PATRICK. *(Tearily.)* No, no, it doesn't. And you know who deserves the blame?

STEVEN. Who?

PATRICK. I blame — myself. At my rapidly advancing age, it behooves me to become a MAN — but I was never given the TOOLS! My mother, that witch, smothering me with her attention, until at seventeen I bolted town so I could BREATHE! And my FATHER! He ALLOWED her to treat me less like a son and more like a sister, and where. Was. He? Watching "the game," that's where! Forever jabbering about PUNTS and YARDS and PENALTIES —

it's as though he were misting the room with faggot repellent! It's no wonder I spend so many lonely nights at the bathhouse, wandering up and down in my towel. Oh Steven, maybe — maybe all those days I spent alone and searching — maybe I was searching for home. Home. At the baths. Home, with nothing of my own but a stale bottle of poppers. Oh, how I hate myself.

STEVEN. No.

PATRICK. I hate myself so very much! Oh, how did I ever end up this way? Oh God, whyyyyyyyy? *(Tesman is trying to sneak past them quietly. Patrick inhales with a huge, dramatic gesture and grabs Tesman's leg in his grief. He suddenly pops up, cheerily, as though nothing had happened.)* Oh, helleeaow!

STEVEN. Don't mind him.

PATRICK. I deliver those cathartic speeches all the time. *(Steven returns Patrick's cocktail to him. They turn in unison and grin at Tesman.)*

STEVEN. Allow me to introduce ourselves. I'm Steven, and she's Patrick. And you are —

TESMAN. Oh, me? I'm — I'm George Tesman. *(They stop.)*

STEVEN. Did you just say —

PATRICK. George Tesman?

TESMAN. Um, I did.

PATRICK. Oh my gosh, we — we love your wife. We're both big fans.

STEVEN. HYUGE.

TESMAN. Oh, gee, thank you. She's awfully special, isn't she? *(He grins uncomfortably.)*

STEVEN. *(To Patrick.)* You know what? I think this fellow's an F.O.D.

PATRICK. Really? *(They regard Tesman a moment.)*

TESMAN. What's that?

PATRICK. An F.O.D. is a Friend Of Dorothy. *(Dorothy Gale from Kansas skips by in the background.)*

PATRICK and STEVEN. Hi Dorothy!

DOROTHY. Hi boys! *(Dorothy waves and exits.)*

TESMAN. I've never seen that girl before in my life!

STEVEN. Well, it's CODE, darling. Patrick and I are homosexuals. Pioneers, really.

TESMAN. What?

STEVEN. We're — what's the word du jour? "Inverts"?

PATRICK. I always liked "Homophiles." "Homosexual" always makes people think of sex.

STEVEN. As though YOU don't always think of sex.

PATRICK. SUCH a bitch today. We both prefer the company of men.

STEVEN. IF you know what we mean.

TESMAN. I'm not sure I do.

PATRICK. Well, in the way you love your Hedda Gabler —

STEVEN. Supposedly —

PATRICK. A man like me could love, say, Steven!

STEVEN. Oh my God, can you imagine?

PATRICK and STEVEN. HAHAHAHAHAHA!

STEVEN. We'd make just the WORST couple.

PATRICK. Imagine ME with HER and her round heels! When the wind changes direction she falls backwards and her legs fly in the air!

PATRICK and STEVEN. HAHAHAHAHA! (They gradually stop laughing. Tesman is troubled.)

TESMAN. I think I strayed too far from home.

PATRICK. Are you heading back?

STEVEN. Take us with you!

PATRICK. We've been DYING to visit the Cul-De-Sac of the Tragic Women!

TESMAN. No, I think I'll press on. Can I ask, though — have you been living here for long?

PATRICK. Steven, I think she's asking our AGE.

STEVEN. The entire Turkish rugby team couldn't drag THAT out of me.

PATRICK. Truth be told, we were created in the glorious year of 1968, and we lived on STAGE, and SCREEN, and …

TESMAN. So far in the future! So THIS is where society is headed!

STEVEN. Yes. Everyone in the future is just like us.

PATRICK. The truth is, Steven and I seem to be a dying breed.

STEVEN. Unfortunately, we have survived DECADES of "future" ourselves.

PATRICK. They hardly ever do our play nowadays.

TESMAN. Why?

PATRICK. Though we're constitutionally on top of the latest trends, I'm afraid we've become rather, well, dated.

STEVEN. They don't make 'em like us any more.

PATRICK. Not to say there aren't homosexuals —

STEVEN. "Fairies!"

PATRICK. "Nancy boys" —

STEVEN. "Sodomites" —

PATRICK. "Fruitcakes" —

STEVEN. "Pillow biters" —

PATRICK. "Fudge packers" —

STEVEN. — or "faggots" —

PATRICK. "Fags," yes, love that —

STEVEN. Whatever you call us, we men-who-love-men are forever POURING out of The Furnace nowadays. Sometimes it's like two-for-one Pink Lady night at the bar, the way we pile up.

PATRICK. But the fags today are such BORES.

STEVEN. They definitely lack a certain elan. We're thinking of moving.

PATRICK. When Steven and I came out of The Furnace, we headed straight to the Immigrants-Filled-With-Hopes-Of-Making-It-In-America Neighborhood and we fixed it right up, and now it's become a homo GHETTO.

STEVEN. And the fags coming out of The Furnace these days won't have a THING to do with us.

PATRICK. One of those nelly modern cows called me "self-hating" the other day!

STEVEN. Well, even when you can't muster the effort, take comfort in the fact that *I* hate you.

PATRICK. *(Fondly.)* And the feeling is mutual. *(They laugh loudly for a moment.)*

STEVEN. But you must understand, we were pioneers!

PATRICK. A sign of PROGRESS! Before we came along, people like us shot ourselves in the HEAD at the ends of our stories!

STEVEN. Patrick.

PATRICK. *(To Tesman.)* I'm sorry. I'm sure in your wife's case it feels very fresh.

STEVEN. But enough about US.

PATRICK. What brings YOU out today? *(They stop and smile at Tesman.)*

TESMAN. I'm actually — I'm off in search of Hedda.

PATRICK. REALLY? Is she OUT here?

TESMAN. Yes, she — she decided she was going to go off in search of — change. And she ran away from me.

STEVEN. Oh dear.

TESMAN. Yes.

PATRICK. And you're going to find her?

TESMAN. I'm going to try.

STEVEN. But what if she doesn't want to come back?

PATRICK. You could stay with us.

TESMAN. I don't know if I'd get along well in the world you fellows live in.

STEVEN. You don't HAVE to be a cocksucker in our world.

PATRICK. Oh yes he does!

TESMAN. A what?

STEVEN. *(To Tesman.)* Oh, you poor thing. You're clearly lost and we're not helping.

PATRICK. I volunteer to help you explore this unfamiliar terrain.

STEVEN. She's a veritable Meriwether Lewis for heterosexual men.

PATRICK. Sacagawea.

STEVEN. Oh right, that's funnier.

PATRICK. You're welcome.

TESMAN. I'm sure I can find my way by myself. It was nice meeting you, um — *(Tesman spots a bit of fabric popping out of Patrick's purse.)* Wait — where did you get THAT?

PATRICK. *(Holding up his purse.)* Oh, this? At the cutest little shop in the Village —

TESMAN. No — that DRESS!

PATRICK. Oh — *(He pulls a bit of the dress out of his bag.)* Someone left their luggage at the head of the trail, and I did a little — recovery.

STEVEN. Theft.

PATRICK. I thought it might be fun to sashay around in this for a theme party. The color goes, don't you think?

TESMAN. That's one of Hedda's dresses. *(Patrick pulls the dress out of his bag. It has an enormous bloodstain.)*

PATRICK. Oh I should have known.

STEVEN. Honey, I told you a billion times, seltzer ain't gonna work on that stain. It's a protein.

PATRICK. Would you stop limiting me?

TESMAN. Where does this trail lead?

PATRICK. Deeper into the Dark Forest.

TESMAN. And what's deeper in the Dark Forest?

PATRICK. It's rather frightening —

STEVEN. — not a bad cruising area —

PATRICK. — and beyond it lies The Furnace.

TESMAN. Dear God — is Hedda going to The Furnace?

STEVEN. I love that name: "The Furnace." It sounds like a gay biker bar.

TESMAN. Would you fellows show me there? Do you mind?

PATRICK. We'd be delighted. *(To Tesman.)* Here, honey, take my arm in case I fall. It's been a bitch breaking in these heels. *(Tesman reluctantly takes Patrick's arm, and they head out.)*

Scene 5

Hedda and Mammy are walking through a dark, gloomy forest. Shadowy figures pass, whispering inaudibly. It's rather frightening. Hedda and Mammy clutch each other in terror.

HEDDA. Mammy, maybe you should walk ahead and scout.

MAMMY. Oh no, Miss Hedda. I's stickin' to you like de tar baby.

HEDDA. No, really, you go ahead. No wandering brigand would dare challenge a woman of your stature.

MAMMY. Oh Miss Hedda, I don' know whatchu get us into dis time. *(Creepy sounds.)*

HEDDA. Mammy, I'm frightened.

MAMMY. Nuttin' frighten you, Miss Hedda. You jus' pretendin' to be frighted 'coz it sound right.

HEDDA. Oh, I'm nothing BUT fear, Mammy! That's why we must press on! *(A bearded man in sandals enters, not seeing them.)*

MAMMY. Who dat?

HEDDA. A beggar man. God knows to what depths he would descend in order to sate his voracious need.

MAMMY. You think he gwynne go hurtin' us?

HEDDA. Why don't you keep watch while I hide.

MAMMY. I's goin' witchu, Miss Hedda. You need protection. *(They hide behind a tree. Mammy sticks out prominently.)*

HEDDA. He can see you. Just so you know.

MAMMY. It's how I's made, Miss Hedda.

JESUS. Good afternoon, sisters.

MAMMY. Oh Lawdy.

HEDDA. Thanks a LOT, Mammy.

JESUS. You have nothing to fear from me, gentle ladies.

MAMMY. Now you be gettin' on, mistah. Git. We ladies out for a nice walk, 'n we's not interested in you's vagranty ways.

JESUS. I will not harm you. I bringeth you soothing blessings from the Lord Our God.

MAMMY. You's a preacher?

JESUS. *(Laughing patiently.)* In a way, good lady. I am the carpenter's son. I am the Prophet. I am Elijah, Rabbi, Teacher, Master, Messiah, the King of the Jews, Son of the Living God, the man Jesus they call the Christ.

MAMMY. Naw, really?

JESUS. Really.

MAMMY. Oh Lawd! I just knows You's around here someplace! I prayin' and prayin' all dese years and here You is! Oh, Miss Hedda, it's the Lawd hisself come to show us de way! *(Hedda steps out from behind the tree, suspiciously.)*

HEDDA. Jesus, heh?

JESUS. Hello, Hedda Gabler. *(Beat.)*

HEDDA. You know my name. Nice trick. But everyone knows MY name. I'm FAMOUS.

JESUS. So am I, Hedda Gabler.

HEDDA. But you're not the REAL Jesus, are you?

JESUS. I'm not the Jesus who walked the earth, if that's what you mean. We are but man's many representations of Jesus. The rest is a matter of your faith.

MAMMY. You said "we."

JESUS. Yes, I did.

MAMMY. You mean dere more den one?

JESUS. Well, of course! After all, right around the corner is the Verdant Glade of the Jesuses! *(The trees perhaps part and let sunlight in.)* Hey, everybody! Come and behold who we've got here! *(Two more Jesuses enter. One of them is a post-crucifixion Jesus, a la Mel Gibson's* The Passion of the Christ. *The other is dressed as a clown.)*

MUSICAL JESUS. Happy returns of the day! Welcome to our village!

SUFFERING JESUS. L'chaim.

JESUS. You'll find hundreds of us here. Feel free to browse until you find the Christ who suits you best. I am closely modeled after the carpenter of the Bible, whose greatest message was to love your neighbor as you yourself would be loved. I suspect that's why I'm one of the less popular Jesuses. Unlike … *(Pointing to Suffering Jesus.)* Jesus here. Now He is for a particular TYPE of person, who's not so much into the NUANCE of things. I swear, His followers seem to RELISH His condition.

SUFFERING JESUS. Those Romans do not mess around. *(The Musical Jesus begins making a balloon hat, humming.)*

JESUS. *(Pointing to Musical Jesus.)* And Musical Jesus is also very popular. We were all a bit surprised when he showed up, but he fits in nicely. *(Musical Jesus places his balloon hat atop Suffering Jesus' crown of thorns. It pops. A Black Jesus enters, waving.)* And Mammy, look who we have here!

MAMMY. There ain't no WAY that be Jesus!

JESUS. You really think so? *(Mammy surveys Black Jesus a moment, suspiciously. Suddenly, she wraps Him in a hug.)*

MAMMY. Thank you, Lord!

JESUS. We're a pretty open-minded lot here. Oh — and look who I found! *(He reaches under a tree and pulls out a baby.)* Look! Awww. This little guy's also very popular. In fact, I'd say *(Holding up the baby.)* this Jesus and *(Pointing to Suffering Jesus.)* this Jesus are by far the two favorites. It's those of us between birth and death who tend to get overlooked.

MAMMY. *(Holding on to Black Jesus.)* Well, I's made MY choice. Ain't that right, Jesus? *(Baby Jesus begins to cry.)* Ohhhh, he be fussin'. Oooooh. Gimme de baby. *(Jesus passes the baby to her, and she takes it expertly.)*

JESUS. I can't imagine a more comforting bosom, Mammy.

MAMMY. *(Blushing.)* Awwww, you's a devil.

JESUS. There's a nice barn over the hill, yonder, if you'd like to put Him down. Jesus will show you The Way. *(Musical Jesus, Black Jesus, and Suffering Jesus lead Mammy out.)*

HEDDA. I'm not sure I'm inclined toward any of you.

JESUS. But certainly, Hedda Gabler, you want to be saved?

HEDDA. I want to cease to exist, altogether.

JESUS. Cease to exist? After all the wonderful gifts showered on you by your creator?

HEDDA. Showered? Ha. Name one.

JESUS. The gift of LIFE, Hedda Gabler.

HEDDA. A MISERABLE life.

JESUS. But LIFE! To exist only in a dream, but more real to your audience than the flesh-and-blood people they hold the dearest!

HEDDA. How is that possible.

JESUS. Because they ENTER you, Hedda. We are not the imaginations of our authors. We are the imaginations of our audience. What a remarkable agreement: One person says "Let me show you a life," and then an audience gathers to say, "Yes, yes, show us a life." And this audience, alone and watching, feels more compassion for the imaginary person in the play or book or film than for the loved one sitting alongside them! It's hysterically improbable but so LOVELY. And this world HUMS from their empathy!

HEDDA. But what life are they watching? The miserable life of a woman trapped. MY life. They can yuk it up all they want, but it's not so fun when you're the object of scrutiny!

JESUS. Not "scrutiny," Hedda: empathy!

HEDDA. People love watching executions, too. You should know.

JESUS. Without us, humanity would ossify. We shake the bark off of people. We keep their imaginations flexible and open to new and life-changing ideas! We will not disappear because the real world does. That world will slow and stop because imagination has died. But The Furnace keeps on churning! For every one of us who is forgotten, another is born to fill the void!

HEDDA. This Furnace — where is it?

JESUS. It's beyond the enormous lake over there. But a delicate creature like you should never behold such horror.

HEDDA. I'm not afraid.

JESUS. I warn you: Only a few of the newcomers survive the birthing process. Most perish in their first moments through a genocide of indifference.

HEDDA. Take me there.

JESUS. What?

HEDDA. If I am to endure against my will, then I must change. And if I can find death, all the better.

JESUS. Hedda, if you're going to The Furnace, you must go alone.

HEDDA. Then alone I will go.

JESUS. No path circumvents the lake. You must go across.

HEDDA. I will swim.

JESUS. But that lovely dress — (A moment. Triumphantly:) Fine! I'll walk you across! (Jesus picks Hedda up as Mammy enters.)

HEDDA. (To Mammy.) Hey Mammy! Jesus is walking me across the lake. You want to come along?

35

MAMMY. I s'pose, Miss Hedda.

JESUS. *(Surveying Mammy's size.)* Um — okay. I'll be right back to get you, Mammy — just as soon as I can. But — I do have this little TWINGE in my back —

MAMMY. I'll be waitin' right here.

JESUS. All right, then. *(Jesus carries Hedda off. Mammy waits a moment, alone, watching them go. She begins to sing, quietly at first, in a rich and powerful voice.)*

MAMMY.
>I mus' walk my lonesome valley
>I got to walk it for myself
>Nobody else kin walk it for me
>I got to walk it for myself
>I must go an stand my trial
>I got to stand it for myself
>Nobody else can stand it for me,
>I got to stand it for myself.

(Musical Jesus enters, with a ukelele.) Hey, Jesus. *(Musical Jesus begins to accompany her.)*

>Jesus cross de river Jordan
>He had to walk it for himself
>Nobody else could walk it for him
>He had to walk it for himself.
>Until I reach-a ma home
>Until I reach-a ma home
>I nevah gon' give de journey ovah
>Until I reach-a ma home
>True believer
>Until I reach-a ma home
>Until I reach-a ma —

(Mammy spies something in the distance.)

>Wait — dere's a boat!

(Waving her arms.)

>Over here! Over here!

(She runs offstage. A few moments pass. Icarus falls from the sky and lands center stage with a heavy thud.)

End of Act One

ACT TWO

Scene 1

The lake. Tesman, Mammy, Steven, and Patrick are in a boat. Tesman is rowing. Mammy, Patrick, and Steven are having a high time. All three have cocktails.

MAMMY. So de entire Yankee army be SWEEPIN' through de town, and SHE sez — an' dis when de baby about to be POPPIN' out — she sez —
STEVEN, PATRICK and MAMMY. "Miz Scarlett, I don' know NOTHIN' bout birthin' babies!" *(They all laugh hard. Mammy pounds the side of the boat in her mirth.)*
STEVEN. Here's how, everybody!
PATRICK and MAMMY. Here's how! *(They toast and drink. Mammy downs her glass to the bottom.)*
PATRICK. My God — do you have a hollow leg? *(Mammy burps. Steven pulls out a shaker and pours Mammy another highball.)*
STEVEN. Here's — to CHANGE, everyone!
PATRICK and MAMMY. To change! *(They all toast and take a big swig.)*
STEVEN. Oh, Lord, I'm getting tight! *(Immediately shutting Patrick down.)* Nyet!
PATRICK. Oooh! I brought a little something! Wanna TURN ON?
STEVEN. Yes, thank you! *(Patrick pulls out a joint and lights it off his cigarette.)*
MAMMY. Turn on what?
STEVEN. Oh, Mammy, you have NO idea what fun we have in the twentieth century.
MAMMY. Things ain't so slow on de plantation. *(She takes a long toke. Patrick turns to Tesman.)*
PATRICK. Excuse me, oarsman? Can you PLEASE accelerate, we'll NEVER make it to the ball in time at the rate you're rowing!

(Patrick, Steven, and Mammy enjoy a long stoned laugh.) Ah, Mammy, what an unexpected pleasure THIS is.

STEVEN. We adore spending time with celebrities.

MAMMY. Oh no, I ain't dat!

STEVEN. You bet your sweet ass you are! You're an ENOR-MOUSLY popular figure.

MAMMY. I is?

PATRICK. Are you kidding? Most people around here would KILL to be as famous as you.

MAMMY. For de life of me I don' know why. Ever'body sez it's shameful to be Mammy. *(She glances nervously at Tesman.)*

PATRICK. Are you all right, milady?

MAMMY. Oh no, I's just fine. *(Something's wrong. Beat.)* Massa Tesman?

TESMAN. Yes?

MAMMY. You arms mus' be gettin' real wore down.

TESMAN. I'm not accustomed to such vigorous exercise.

MAMMY. Why don'tchu come and sit yosself down and let me do some rowin'.

TESMAN. Oh, gee, just in time. *(Tesman stops rowing and trades places with Mammy. Patrick and Steven shriek in terror as the boat rocks. Mammy begins to row. Tesman settles.)* That rowing is exhausting work, I say! Phew! *(He grins uneasily. Beat. Patrick and Steven glance back at the vigorously rowing Mammy.)*

PATRICK. I feel oogy.

STEVEN. Me too.

PATRICK. The shadow of human enslavement has crashed our lovely fete.

MAMMY. *(Not paying attention, singing to herself:)* "Ol' Man River ... " *(The Woman in Pink floats by in an innertube. She sees Mammy rowing, and shakes her head. Mammy sees her and waves, wanly. The Woman in Pink drifts away.)*

PATRICK. Well now I feel downright oppressive. Mammy?

MAMMY. Yassum?

PATRICK. I won't allow you to row a scant moment longer!

MAMMY. Oh Lawd, I's just fine.

PATRICK. No, really, darling, you've slaved enough for one day.

STEVEN. Lifetime.

PATRICK. Come back to the fore. Have another cocktail.

MAMMY. Oh no, I ain't lettin' YOU row, Massa Patrick! See, I's just fine. Happy as kin be.

PATRICK. Two things. One: I'm not your "massa." And two: I didn't say I was going to row. George, get back up there.

TESMAN. *(Unenthused.)* Why me?

PATRICK. Because you're so strong.

STEVEN. Oh, yes. I do feel so CARED FOR when he's at the helm.

PATRICK. His rippling muscles —

STEVEN. Clenching and clutching —

PATRICK. The sweat glistening on his brow —

STEVEN. As he labors for his brood —

TESMAN. Oh, you fellows. Really? You see muscles?

PATRICK and STEVEN. YES!

TESMAN. Mammy? *(Tesman trades places with Mammy. Patrick and Steven scream again as the boat rocks. Mammy returns to the front of the boat uneasily. Tesman resumes rowing.)*

MAMMY. I feels all wrong.

STEVEN. Luxuriate! Like this! *(He luxuriates. Mammy shakes her head.)*

MAMMY. I know I's old-fashioned.

PATRICK. *(Fixing a drink for Mammy.)* No, a gin ricky is "old-fashioned." Remaining a virgin until marriage is "old-fashioned." "Old-fashioned" implies a quaint fustiness, which isn't quite the same as being someone's SLAVE. *(Steven pulls out a soda gun attached to a hose, and splashes soda in Patrick's drink. Patrick hands the drink to Mammy.)*

MAMMY. I's jist not from dese times. I's a relic, dey say.

STEVEN. Oh, join the club. Our entire GENERATION is considered shameful.

MAMMY. Why be dat?

STEVEN. They consider us an embarrassing reminder of the bad old days.

PATRICK. Steven and I are situated on the awkward end of a pivotal moment. Society was on the verge of making an ENORMOUS step forward, and we were the first wave of troops to land at Normandy.

STEVEN. We arrived at the party while the hosts were still setting up.

MAMMY. I knows dat feelin'!

STEVEN. Oh, to survive with grace!

PATRICK. To escape the prison of timeliness!

STEVEN. To be —

PATRICK and STEVEN. Hedda Gabler!

PATRICK. Imagine.

MAMMY. But dere nobody more unhappy den Miss Hedda.

PATRICK. Really?

STEVEN. She has NO idea how lucky she is!

PATRICK. If I had that kind of longevity I'd be dancing in the streets!

STEVEN. And short of that he minces. *(Patrick pulls Steven's hair.)* Ow!

PATRICK. I mean, aside from her propensity for destroying people, the suicides, etcetera, Hedda Gabler really should be grateful.

MAMMY. But if Miss Hedda be's happy, den she stop bein' Miss Hedda.

STEVEN. And if you stopped being a slave ...

MAMMY. ... den I stop bein' Mammy.

PATRICK. And if I didn't spout such snappy dialogue I wouldn't be a dated faggot.

STEVEN. Then shut your pie-hole! Spare us all!

PATRICK. Fuck you, Steven.

STEVEN. Fuck you.

PATRICK. See, that's how we ARE. Forever SNIPING. God, I hate ourselves!

MAMMY. I ain't too fond of myself, neider.

PATRICK. What about you, Tesman?

TESMAN. Hm? Sorry, I'm reflecting on the ancient arts and crafts movement of the Brabant region. What were you asking?

PATRICK. *(To Steven.)* You were right from the start. This one isn't sexy AT ALL. *(A moment.)* I know. Let's play a game.

STEVEN. Oh God. That always elevates the party.

MAMMY. What kinna game?

PATRICK. In this game, all you have to do is answer a simple yes-or-no question.

MAMMY. Sho.

PATRICK. And the question is this: If you could become part of the society that oppresses you — would you do it? You first, Mammy. *(Beat.)*

MAMMY. I jes don' know. I don' know how it is bein' somebody else.

PATRICK. Then you have a pass until the next round. It's my

turn. *(A moment.)* I would.

STEVEN. You'd be straight?

PATRICK. Yes.

STEVEN. Then you're a coward.

PATRICK. But I would. *(Beat.)*

STEVEN. So would I.

MAMMY. Yassum, I s'pose I'd change myself too. *(They all sigh. A moment.)*

PATRICK. Sorry, Mammy. All of our parties end like this. *(They row off.)*

Scene 2

The Furnace. A terrifying, burned-out place, filled with smoke and scored by a Carmina Burana-style soundtrack. The area is stacked high with dead bodies. Placed in the audience, unseen, is a giant, flaming furnace. It glows a fiery red. Eilert Lovborg huddles in the midst of the carnage, looking out. Hedda enters. Seeing The Furnace, she falls to the ground in horror. A woman emerges from the audience, screaming.

DYING WOMAN. Help me! Won't you please help me!

HEDDA. Can you tell me — is this The Furnace?

DYING WOMAN. Please — I'm dying! My heart! I'm fading away! The world is turning black!

HEDDA. What happened?

DYING WOMAN. I don't know! I just came out of — out of that HELLFIRE! Oh my God!

HEDDA. Who are you?

DYING WOMAN. *(Miserably:)* I'm a spunky single mom with three wisecracking kids! And my life is supposed to be HILARI-OUS! But not now! Not HERE! Oh, look at all the people! Look at all the DEATH! *(She dies at Hedda's feet. Hedda disengages herself. She wanders through the carnage and sees Lovborg. She goes to him.)*

HEDDA. Lovborg! Eilert Lovborg! *(No response.)* Eilert, it's me! It's Hedda — Hedda Gabler! *(He pushes her away.)* I came all this

41

way to see you! *(A junkie emerges from the audience.)*

JUNKIE. Hey! Hey, man! Hey, man, c'mon gimme some sugar. C'mon, man, I just came outta there, and damn do I need a fix! Some smack! C'mon, just give me some smack! I have AIDS! I need my horse! I'll fuck you!

HEDDA. Get off of me! *(She throws the junkie aside violently. She dies.)* Please — Eilert, stop staring at that! Look at me!

LOVBORG. *(Eyes forward.)* Go home, Hedda Gabler.

HEDDA. No, no, Eilert — I'm — I suppose I — you see, I came all this way because — I'm trying to express my — my —

LOVBORG. Apologies?

HEDDA. I — I want to apologize, but —

LOVBORG. But you can't.

HEDDA. I can SAY I'm sorry but I don't know if I feel it.

LOVBORG. You destroyed my masterwork, Hedda. You made me start drinking again. You gave me a gun to kill myself. You destroyed the lives of everyone around you by shooting yourself in the head.

HEDDA. All RIGHT. I'm SORRY.

LOVBORG. Really?

HEDDA. No. Maybe. I guess not.

LOVBORG. You can't be sorry, Hedda. It's not in your nature.

HEDDA. God DAMN my nature! Eilert, if I could only change it, I would. Stop staring into that horrible thing!

LOVBORG. The Furnace is all there is, Hedda Gabler.

HEDDA. Oh, stop being so ARTSY. It's a BORE. Where is my Eilert? My Eilert with the vine leaves in his hair?

LOVBORG. That man never existed. I was created as I am.

HEDDA. God DAMN that playwright.

LOVBORG. Ibsen, yes.

HEDDA. What?

LOVBORG. Henrik Ibsen. The playwright who created us.

HEDDA. What I wouldn't give to meet him! Oh, to wrap my fingers around his neck!

LOVBORG. You were one of his biggest successes.

HEDDA. I was never ASKED. I think that galls me the most.

LOVBORG. And because of Ibsen we will never die. Amidst this horror, we persist.

HEDDA. Oh the bodies, the way they pile up!

LOVBORG. It is all there is, Hedda. Gaze into it. You are looking into the mouth of our God.

HEDDA. But the violence! These people — these poor, invented people, emerging with such hope in their faces — and then so many, so many collapse — and die —

LOVBORG. Look into The Furnace, Hedda Gabler, and feel lucky to be alive.

HEDDA. But I cannot go on living. Help me, Eilert. *(A moment.)*

LOVBORG. You wish to forget your pain.

HEDDA. Oh, so much!

LOVBORG. You gave me a gift, Hedda Gabler. Remember?

HEDDA. What gift.

LOVBORG. This. *(He pulls out a pistol.)* Take it. Use it. It's yours. You gave it to me. A loan of sorts. *(He hands her the gun.)* You can forget your pain.

HEDDA. But always in time the world reassembles and I'm right in the middle of it!

LOVBORG. But before your world reassembles, you have a few rare moments of obliviousness and confusion.

HEDDA. Oh, yes, yes — I remember — it was joyous, joyous compared to this. *(She goes to him.)* Eilert — please, we can have a life together.

LOVBORG. You will destroy me sooner or later, Hedda Gabler.

HEDDA. Only you can save me.

LOVBORG. You'll destroy me.

HEDDA. *(Frustrated.)* Oh probably, but so what?

LOVBORG. Only Ibsen can save you, Hedda Gabler.

HEDDA. Where is he?

LOVBORG. *(Pointing into The Furnace.)* In there. All creativity is inside.

HEDDA. But I can't go in there, Eilert! It must be ten thousand degrees!

LOVBORG. Then kill yourself or turn toward home.

HEDDA. Coming here was my only hope. *(She stares out, sadly. We hear the screams of the dying. Mammy enters, and stops when she sees the carnage. She surveys the area.)*

MAMMY. Well I'll be. I don' see no Mammys noplace. Dey sho ain't makin' my kind no mo. *(Mammy walks to the front of the stage and stares out. Steven and Patrick enter, and reel back.)*

PATRICK. Oh my God!

STEVEN. It's a GIANT FLAMING VAGINA! *(Tesman enters.)*

TESMAN. Hedda! Hedda!

HEDDA. Oh, God! Tesman, go home!

TESMAN. Hedda — I brought your gun — oh, you HAVE a gun! Well, here's the other one. *(He hands her his gun. She holds a pistol in each hand.)*

HEDDA. Why does everybody want me to kill myself?

STEVEN. Oh, YES! Would you? *(Summoning Patrick, clapping excitedly.)* Patrick, Patrick, it's HER! And she has GUNS!

PATRICK. *(Rushing up.)* I just want to say … it's such an honor meeting you, Miss Gabler. *(Steven poses beside Hedda, and Patrick snaps a flash photo.)*

HEDDA. Who ARE you people?

MAMMY. Now you don' go killin' yoself, Miss Hedda. You sit tight. Somebody gotta find out what be in dere and it may as well be Mammy.

HEDDA. What do you mean?

MAMMY. I ain' come dis far to turn back now. I gon' see this journey to de very end.

HEDDA. But Mammy — this IS the end!

MAMMY. Oh no it ain't. *(She hikes up her petticoats.)* Mammy's goin' in. *(Everyone responds in shock and horror. Mammy charges up the aisle toward The Furnace.)*

PATRICK. Be careful, Mammy! You'll get singed!

STEVEN. I can't watch!

PATRICK. Mammy, Mammy stop!

HEDDA. Will one of you act like a MAN and STOP her?

PATRICK. *(To Lovborg.)* Yes! Stop her!

STEVEN. She's — she's going inside!

PATRICK. Oh, ouch! *(Mammy's gone. We hear a horrible echoing, burning, apocalyptic sound. A moment.)* Well, there's that.

HEDDA. Will she be all right?

LOVBORG. I don't know. I've sat here for decades and I thought I'd seen every possible kind of behavior. But I never saw anybody try that.

HEDDA. And she left me all alone to fend for myself! Oh, Eilert, what about ME? What will I do?

LOVBORG. It takes courage to shoot yourself, Hedda. It's perhaps the only courageous act you've ever performed.

TESMAN. Yes, yes, darling. You can use either gun. If you use Eilert's, I won't be offended.

HEDDA. My death was the act of ultimate cowardice.

STEVEN. But THRILLING onstage. Really. I wish you could have seen it from the audience, just once. *(Shouting, off.)* MAMMY. MAMMY. ARE YOU ALL RIGHT? *(No response.)* She can't possibly be dead, can she?

PATRICK. I'm going to miss Mammy. She was a scream.

HEDDA. Eilert — you said this Ibsen person was in there.

LOVBORG. All creation is inside, Hedda Gabler.

HEDDA. *(Gazing at her pistols.)* One brave act. One brave and beautiful act.

TESMAN. Yes, Hedda — yes — *(A moment. Hedda throws down her pistols.)*

HEDDA. I'm going inside.

TESMAN. Whatever for?

HEDDA. To change! I am gonna find that Henrik Ibsen and make him revise my life! *(Hedda starts into The Furnace.)*

TESMAN. Hedda, no! Stop! *(A helpless moment.)* Hedda. *(Patrick turns to Steven.)*

PATRICK. Let's follow them! Wouldn't that be a camp?

STEVEN. Why on earth?

PATRICK. Maybe WE can change, too!

STEVEN. And then what?

PATRICK. I could at the very least fix my "S" problem. *(Practicing:)* "S." No. "S." No.

STEVEN. I'm not going in there.

PATRICK. Stop being such a princess. What's it my gym teacher used to always say? "Grow a pair" or something. Well, Steven, GROW A PAIR.

STEVEN. You sound more like my choir teacher.

PATRICK. It'll be a kick! Come on!

STEVEN. Patrick, people may say our lifestyle is a choice, but GIVEN the choice I still don't see myself longing after — you know, "breasts" — in a convincing way.

PATRICK. But we can change our very natures! We won't care what we're missing! *(Running up the aisle:)* Last one in's a dated homosexual! *(He stops, and waits a moment.)* A lonely, self-hating, bitter, jaded, AGING —

STEVEN. All right! I'm coming!

PATRICK. Hooray! Here we go…! *(They hold hands and follow Hedda into The Furnace. A series of horrible echoing burning sounds as the fire flares. Tesman sits quietly next to Eilert, and they stare into The Furnace.)*

TESMAN. They're gone.

LOVBORG. Yes, George Tesman.

TESMAN. No wonder people shun this place. The carnage! We're sitting in the midst of a war.

LOVBORG. I can think of no more beautiful sight than this. Ungainly and bloody and flowering. Forever flowering.

TESMAN. If you say so, Eilert. *(They stare into The Furnace.)*

Scene 3

The apocalyptic sounds of The Furnace rise, then fade. The stage is plunged into darkness. Mammy appears.

MAMMY. Hello? Hello? Lawdy, if it ain't dark in here! If I be inside de head of dat writer lady, dere ain't much goin' on, dat fo sho. *(Mammy disappears, and Hedda appears, in a different area of the stage. She squints into the lights.)*

HEDDA. Mr. Ibsen? Hello? It's me, Hedda Gabler. I know you're still working on my play, and I can only imagine how hard it must be when you're such a "creative person," coming up with all of your neat ideas. That being said, I've been thinking about the ending, and I have a few notes. *(Lights shift to Mammy.)*

MAMMY. *(We hear a bird, chirping. Mammy inhales.)* But wait. De grass done been cut. Dat smell in de airs — it be familiar. De horse droppins, and de barbecue — Wait — I mus' be back on de plantation! *(We hear "Swing Low, Sweet Chariot" in the distance.)*

FEMALE VOICE. *(Very shrill and Southern, off.)* Mammy! Mammy! I need help gettin' on my dress for the cotillion! *(Mammy sighs. Lights shift to Hedda.)*

HEDDA. So what about THIS — if we go from right before I fire the gun, when I'm offstage — let me show you. *(A curtain appears. Hedda runs behind it.)* I hear everything you're saying, Tesman! But what about me? What am I supposed to do at home all alone?

TESMAN. *(Suddenly appearing.)* Well — the Judge will peek in every now and then, won't you Judge?

JUDGE BRACK. *(Suddenly appearing.)* With happiness. Every

night. We'll get along just dandily.

HEDDA. *(Offstage.)* Do you think so, Judge? Really? Now that you're the big shot? *(A loud gunshot, followed by silence.)*

TESMAN. That Hedda and her pistols! Darling, really — *(He pulls the curtain back. Hedda stands, aiming her pistol out a window.)*

HEDDA. Sorry everybody, that pesky stray was getting into the trash again. *(Lights on Mammy.)*

FEMALE VOICE. *(Offstage.)* Mammy, come lace me into my corset or I'll be ever so cross!

MAMMY. Sho 'nuff, I's comin'.

FEMALE VOICE. *(Offstage.)* Oh, fiddle-dee-dee, Mammy, can't you hurry?

MAMMY. I says, I's — *(A little musical sting. Mammy stops.)* Hold on, Mammy. You gotta take dis writer lady by de neck. 'Cuz I ain' goin' back out in de world until — until somethin' be changin' 'roun' heah. 'Cuz I ain't gwynne be no steeryotype no mo. You heah me, Miss Writer Lady?

FEMALE VOICE. *(Offstage.)* MAMMY! MY CORSET!

MAMMY. *(Snarling.)* LACE DAT DAMN CORSET ON YOSELF!

FEMALE VOICE. *(Offstage.)* What? What did you dare say to me?

MAMMY. I SAYS, DO IT YOSELF! AN' I'S TELLING YOU, I AIN' GOIN! *(A gentle musical refrain begins. Hedda holds Tesman and Brack's hands.)*

HEDDA. And deep in my heart I believe we really must love, all of us, each other. For if we all try — really try to be happy, if we work, and we must work, if we work we will succeed someday. Some day we will find happiness, all of us, together. *(Mammy sings:)*

MAMMY.
> HERE I IS
> HERE I IS
> ON DE EDGE OF SOMETHIN' NEW.

HEDDA. We must look to the future, the future generations, whose lives we shall never know.

MAMMY.
> DOWN AND OUT
> I'S WORKIN' ALL DE TIME
> I SO TIRED OF FEELIN' BLUE.

HEDDA. We'll turn from sadness and anger, and treat each other with dignity and, yes, love.

MAMMY.
   BUT WHEN I'S CREATED
   I DIN' GET EDUCATED
   AND IT LOOK LIKE MY LIFE GON' BE LONG —
HEDDA. For though today may be awful, tomorrow — tomorrow is another day! (Hedda, Tesman, and the Judge stare beatifically in the distance.)
MAMMY.
   WHO'D LIVE FOREVER AT DIS KINNA PRICE?
   I JIS' DON' KNOW WHAT I DONE WRONG.
(Hedda's scene disappears, leaving Mammy alone. She takes center stage.)
   HERE I IS
   HERE I IS
   I BE SIMPLE, SO DEY SAY
   I LEARN A WORD
   I NEVER HEAR BEFORE
   WHEN DEY CALL ME A "CLICHE"
   BUT DAT GON' BE CHANGIN'
   YEAH! I'S GWYNNE BE CHANGIN!
   NO MO FEELIN' SAD AND FORLORN
   'CUZ LISTEN UP, YOU!
   I WON'T BE YO JIGABOO!
   I'S COME BACK TO DE DAY I WAS BORN!

   SO LOOK OUT MOMMY, MAMMY'S HERE TO TAKE
      CHARGE
   DROP DEM SHACKLES AND DEM APRON STRINGS!
   I'S GWYNNE START LIVIN' AND I'S GONNA LIVE
      LARGE
   I AIN'T GWYNNE BE NO WIND 'NEATH YOUR WINGS

   I BE ESCAPIN'!
   I'S GONNA FIND FAME!
   I'S STARTIN' A SINGIN' CAREER!
   I WAN' A NEW BODY AND I WAN' A NEW NAME
   GUESS WHAT? SHAMARI ROBINSON'S —
(In an instant, Mammy has transformed. She wears a sparkly, torchy dress and a feathered hat. A chorus joins in. They may be onstage behind her, or can sing off:)
HERE — I — AM!

CHORUS.
  HERE SHE IS!
MAMMY.
  HERE I AM!
CHORUS.
  HERE SHE IS! AAAHH-AHHH …
MAMMY.
  RESPLENDENT IN MY MAJESTY!
  I HAVE DREAMS!
CHORUS.
  SHE HAS DREAMS!
MAMMY.
  I HAVE A STORY!
CHORUS.
  AND A STORY!
MAMMY.
  AND IT'S NOT ABOUT WHITEY!
CHORUS.
  NOT WHITEY NO, AAHHH …
MAMMY.
  SO LOOK OUT WORLD, MAMMY'S GONE WITH THE
    WIND
  AND I'LL STAND CENTER AND TAKE A BOW
CHORUS.
  YOU TAKE THAT BOW, AAAHH …
MAMMY.
  I REWROTE MY HISTORY AND I'M CHANGING MY
    LIFE
  AND
MAMMY AND CHORUS.
  NOBODY CAN STOP — ME — NOW!

Scene 4

Outside The Furnace. Shamari stands center-stage, looking fabulous. Across the stage stands Hedda, gasping for air.

HEDDA. *(To herself.)* I made it out of The Furnace!

SHAMARI. You most certainly did.

HEDDA. I feel BOUNCY! Oh, gee! *(To Shamari.)* I'm sorry to bother you. But can I ask you a question?

SHAMARI. Of course.

HEDDA. Do I look happy to you? If you saw me on a stage, say, would you look at me and think, "Now there's a happy woman!"?

SHAMARI. That's just what I would think.

HEDDA. Then — it is done. All complications are settled. The truth, confronted. A better world beckons! I can live — I can live forever, now, and be happy.

SHAMARI. Me too. *(Hedda's in a happy reverie, beaming in wonderment.)* You don't recognize me, do you?

HEDDA. I don't think so.

SHAMARI. You sure?

HEDDA. *(Recognizing her.)* Oh no!

SHAMARI. Oh yes.

HEDDA. Mammy?

SHAMARI. Not anymore. My name is Shamari Robinson.

HEDDA. Mammy?

SHAMARI. Shamari.

HEDDA. I can't believe it's you! You're so ARTICULATE!

SHAMARI. *(Patiently.)* Thank you.

HEDDA. We wrestled with Fate and came out the victors! Oh, Mammy!

SHAMARI. Shamari.

HEDDA. Oh, hold me, Mammy.

SHAMARI. Honey, let's get one thing straight, all right?

HEDDA. What.

SHAMARI. Mammy's gone.

HEDDA. Sorry. Shamari. *(She bursts into giggles. She whoops in joy*

50

and jumps up and down like a little girl. She cries excitedly to the skies, ricocheting around the stage in celebration.) Oh, finally, to feel happiness BLASTING through my veins! To drink in the simple joy of being alive — a joy that common people take for granted! And it was so EASY, really —

SHAMARI. Easy?

HEDDA. Oh, yes, after passing through the threshold, I was actually living inside the fermenting brilliance of my creator's imagination! And he wanted my story to end without melancholy — he did! And at last — I felt power to shape my own destiny! I felt, for the first time, I could change the course of my life. And — *(She makes a "ta da!" gesture.)* Look at me! Happy, and — yes, SENSITIVE, Mammy! I am a feeling person!

SHAMARI. Congratulations.

HEDDA. Thank you.

SHAMARI. And I'm sure you're very curious about me.

HEDDA. Oh, of course, yes, sure.

SHAMARI. Well, I made the plantation back home into a hub of the Underground Railroad. And then I hightailed it outta there to New York, and became an internationally famous chanteuse. In the process I laid the groundwork for a musical style known as Jazz. At last I died at a dignified old age in the Utopian Socialist collective I founded, surrounded by my five children, thirteen grandchildren, ex-lovers, adoring fans, and my loyal white maid Ethel. *(A moment.)*

HEDDA. Gee, I wish I'd thought of that for my ending! *(Tesman enters, a bit woozily.)*

TESMAN. Hedda?

HEDDA. George!

TESMAN. I found you. *(She hugs him.)*

HEDDA. My darling George, it's time to laugh and live and love together. My funny, funny little man of books — we're truly a mismatched pair — but our differences now, they can be the stuff of comedy! Fetching, whimsical fun!

TESMAN. Hedda, I need to sit down.

HEDDA. Of course, George. *(To Shamari.)* Well, I do believe, after our exhausting journey, it's time to turn back home.

SHAMARI. Y'all travel safe, now.

HEDDA. You make it sound as if you're not coming with us!

SHAMARI. Yes, that'd be about right.

HEDDA. But —

SHAMARI. I'm going back where I belong — with my people.

HEDDA. But WE'RE your people!

SHAMARI. Not anymore.

HEDDA. But Mammy, I'd come to depend on you!

SHAMARI. Yes, you most certainly did.

HEDDA. Wouldn't you miss me?

SHAMARI. I'll have to shoulder that burden and carry on. *(Patrick and Steven enter.)*

PATRICK. Well, that was certainly INTERESTING, wasn't it?

STEVEN. I liked our writer.

PATRICK. Me too! A total sweetheart. I feel utterly refreshed and ready to handle the next several decades. *(He spots Hedda. To Patrick:)* Oh, look out — Miss Gabler has returned.

HEDDA. *(Seeing them.)* Ahoy there, fellas! Boy, am I glad to see you guys! Welcome back! *(She gives both of them a hug. Patrick and Steven accept it with shock.)* You boys look terrific. I love that turtleneck on you.

PATRICK. Oh dear.

STEVEN. Oh no.

PATRICK. Honey, what HAPPENED?

HEDDA. I changed my ending. I want — to live! *(They stare at her, stunned, for a moment. Steven slaps Hedda.)*

PATRICK. Steven!

STEVEN. It's the only way I can handle stress.

HEDDA. Why did you slap me?

PATRICK. Because you can't DO that!

HEDDA. Do what?

STEVEN. Hug us and get all sentimental!

PATRICK. Are you CRAZY, woman?

HEDDA. What? Why not? *(Tesman falls over, and lies motionless. Nobody notices. Hedda loses her balance for a moment.)* Whoa, I'm feeling a little dizzy. *(She swoons. Steven catches her. Shamari runs over and takes her other arm.)*

STEVEN. *(To Shamari.)* Oh — thank you, Miss, um — *(Steven recognizes Shamari, and screams.)* Oh God, Patrick, LOOK!

PATRICK. Sweet Suffering Jesu! What have you DONE?

SHAMARI. What do you mean what have I done?

STEVEN. You can't just go turning all fabulous when you started out as MAMMY!

SHAMARI. Watch me. I'm setting an honorable precedent. *(She swoons, a bit.)* Oh Lord, I don't feel so good.

PATRICK. Of course you don't feel good! People don't want to SEE an HONORABLE PRECEDENT!

STEVEN. God, no. They want UNHAPPY people!

PATRICK. Miserable, conflicted wretches who are fighting for their lives! *(He sees Tesman. To Steven:)* Steven, look! We'd better hustle these three back into The Furnace, STAT, or it's gonna look like the end of *Hamlet* around here.

STEVEN. Yes, Doctor. *(Steven gets Hedda up. Patrick goes to George and shakes him.)*

PATRICK. George, George, get your ass up and follow that faggot. Go!

TESMAN. Unggh … *(Steven gets George up.)*

STEVEN. Come on, you two. Nurse Steve is gonna fix you RIGHT up.

PATRICK. Wait, I want to be the nurse! *(Steven pulls them back into The Furnace.)*

HEDDA. *(Slurring loudly as she exits.)* OH GOD, WHY CAN'T I EVER BE HAPPY? *(Patrick and Shamari are alone.)*

PATRICK. Honey, we need to talk.

SHAMARI. Go right ahead. I'm gonna sit down here for a minute and catch my breath.

PATRICK. No, nyet, get up. You're DYING.

SHAMARI. Oh I am not, I'm feeling just — *(She has a coughing fit.)*

PATRICK. I know you've had it with bossy white people, but listen to me: You gotta go back in there and change your story back!

SHAMARI. Oh no I don't.

PATRICK. But the "new you" is a FAILURE! A turkey! A flop!

SHAMARI. Who says?

PATRICK. Hello? You've got the plague!

SHAMARI. It's just a cold.

PATRICK. We don't get colds here unless we're from an ANACIN commercial. You've got the deadly virus of unpopularity! *(A moment.)*

SHAMARI. If that's the case, I'm gonna stay out here just the way I am.

PATRICK. Stay out HERE? And DIE?

SHAMARI. You heard me.

PATRICK. Don't you dare deprive the world of Mammy!

SHAMARI. You just wanna see a Negro woman bowing and grinning with her teeth all white and her eyes rolling and talking that funny slave talk. Well, not me. I'm gonna be a credit to my race. I'm not adding to the misery of the world. *(Shamari begins gasping painfully for air.)*

PATRICK. But misery is the air we BREATHE, all of us. You can't just wish it away! Steven and I could have changed ourselves when WE went into our writer's head, but we didn't!

SHAMARI. Why not?

PATRICK. Well, there was an open bar. But also — we met all kinds of fascinating homosexuals who had yet to be created — and we realized that we may be dated, but we're a foothold for better times to come. And Mammy is too! Your audience needs her!

SHAMARI. *(Gesturing toward the audience.)* My audience? Screw my audience. Every single one of 'em. If I'm easier to swallow when I'm shucking and jiving, then they can *go ahead and choke.*

PATRICK. But we are the shadow history of the world. You, and me and Steven, and Hedda — and — oh, God, I wonder how she's doing in there — *(A gunshot, off. Clapping.)* Oh, yay! *(He stops clapping.)* Sorry. *(A moment.)* You know what? You might hate me for this, but I think Mammy was a wonderful character. A stereotype, yes, but a damned good character. And I'm not going to sit here and watch you die. I'll just go. Because nobody loves a martyr. *(To himself.)* Oh, that is SO not true. Okay, I'll stay. *(He sits by her and pats her hand.)* Be brave, my darling. Be brave. Enter the light. *(He begins to cry. Shamari looks at him, wearily.)* FINE, I'll go. I'm not very good at these inspirational-type discussions. I'm not designed that way. *(He takes a few steps, and turns.)* We're baby steps. We're the pioneers. *(Shamari nods, very sick. Patrick goes. Shamari sits, alone, her breath getting increasingly labored.)*

Scene 5

We find Hedda, alone.

HEDDA. Surely, if my life here were a story, then this would be the point of rescue. Or of being set adrift. Of anything final, I can't say I care. But instead — I have to endure. Is this how it feels to be real? To live your life, dreaming of some deus ex machina that's never going to come? *(She looks off.)* You said we were going home. *(Patrick and Steven appear.)*

STEVEN. We'll be home soon enough. But we thought we'd make a final side-trip.

HEDDA. Where is this place?

PATRICK. This is the Subdivision of the Eternal Audience.

STEVEN. We come here, sometimes, when we need a lift.

PATRICK. You've never been? *(Hedda shakes her head.)* Oh, it's fabulous. You can see every production going on in the outside world. Sometimes two and three different performances of the same story, all going on at once.

STEVEN. It's a horn-o-plenty for theater queens.

PATRICK. *(Pointing in the distance.)* Oh look — see — there's a *King Lear* in Swahili, beside a cruise-ship version of *A Chorus Line*, and next to that is a third-grade production of something about a pony — it's mad! None of the actors are aware of each other, or us, and it's just DIVINE —

STEVEN. The other day we watched the WORST *Auntie Mame*.

PATRICK. YES.

STEVEN. Done by a community theater somewhere in Wisconsin, I believe.

PATRICK. Totally inept.

STEVEN. 'Cause we KNOW Mame, of course —

PATRICK. We're dear chums, really —

STEVEN. "Bosom buddies" —

PATRICK. *(To Steven.)* Thank you —

STEVEN. — and compared to the lady we know and adore, the actress portraying Auntie Mame — ugh!

PATRICK. Pretty slim pickin's at HER banquet.

STEVEN. She was like a saleslady for euthanasia.

PATRICK. We thought it might be nice for you to see someone else's story.

STEVEN. Or you could see your own, too, if you wanted.

HEDDA. Why on earth would I want to see myself?

STEVEN. Oh, it's great fun, actually. Once, we saw our play done by an avant-garde marionette theater, and it was a gas. *(Patrick peers through some opera glasses.)*

PATRICK. Oh, look! See — I TOLD you there was a *Hedda Gabler* going on over here. Look! Look! *(The curtain opens to reveal a performance of* Hedda Gabler. *It begins in pantomime. Note: A different set of actors play the roles. "George Tesman" and "Thea Elvsted" sit together at a desk, poring over some papers. "Judge Brack" sits in a side chair, looking smug. Beside him stands "Hedda." The actress wears extremely heavy makeup and a dress that serves up generous cleavage. "Hedda" and "Judge Brack" speak in hushed tones, pretending to have a relaxing chat. [Dialogue from the pantomimed scene between Hedda and the Judge can be found in the Appendix.])* Oh, but it's practically over.

HEDDA. Who are THEY?

STEVEN. This is YOUR PLAY, darling!

HEDDA. *(Recoiling.)* Oh, no, eck! *(Unable to help herself.)* Wait — which one's which?

STEVEN. *(Pointing to the actors.)* Well, that's Thea Elvsted there sitting at the desk, and next to her is your husband —

HEDDA. HAH HAH HAH! Look at Tesman's glasses! That's a riot!

PATRICK. And this must be Judge Brack standing over there —

HEDDA. Oh, yes, he looks dreadful. Perfect.

PATRICK. *(Pointing to the "Hedda" actress.)* And this is — well, this is — *(An uncomfortable moment as Hedda surveys the actress' heavy makeup and low-cut dress.)*

HEDDA. Please tell me this is Diana, the randy town prostitute.

PATRICK. I think this is you.

HEDDA. What do you mean, me?

PATRICK. This is the actress playing you.

HEDDA. NOOOOOOOOO! That isn't FAIR!

PATRICK. Squint your eyes a bit. It's like filming through gauze.

HEDDA. Don't I get any approval over casting? This is horrible!

STEVEN. Maybe she's married to the artistic director.

PATRICK. I saw her when she played "Peter Pan" last season. She's really not so bad.

STEVEN. Now ssshhhh, let's pay attention. *(Patrick pulls out a crinkly candy and opens it crinklingly.)* Put that away. *(The actors become audible.)*

"HEDDA GABLER." So I'm completely under your thumb. Forever.

"JUDGE BRACK." I promise you, I won't abuse my position.

"HEDDA GABLER." I can't bear the thought. I can't. At your beck and call, forever in your power —

"JUDGE BRACK." One grows accustomed to such things.

"HEDDA GABLER." Perhaps they do. *("Hedda" gets up and goes calmly to "George.")* How's the new project going, Tesman?

"GEORGE TESMAN." Oh Lord, we'll be at this for months — perhaps years!

"HEDDA GABLER." Imagine that. *(She turns to Thea.)* Isn't it funny, Thea, now you're sitting with George the same way you sat with Eilert Lovborg!

"THEA ELVSTED." If only I could inspire your husband in the same way!

"HEDDA GABLER." I have no doubt you will, in time.

"GEORGE TESMAN." It's so funny, Hedda — because I feel it happening already! Darling, go talk some more with the Judge. *("Hedda" turns to "Judge Brack," who smiles cruelly. She turns back.)*

"HEDDA GABLER." So I can't be useful to any of you?

"GEORGE TESMAN." No, darling.

HEDDA. This is where it turns. *(The real Hedda watches the actors intently, moving to the stage and standing right beside them.)*

"GEORGE TESMAN." *(To "Judge Brack":)* Judge, I hope you'll keep Hedda good company from now on.

"JUDGE BRACK." I'd be delighted.

"HEDDA GABLER." *(Not looking at him.)* Thank you. *("Hedda Gabler" stands, frozen. The real Hedda goes to her, standing right beside her, watching her intently.)* I feel tired tonight.

HEDDA. Oh God!

"HEDDA GABLER." I'm going to go lie down in there for a bit. On the sofa.

"GEORGE TESMAN." Yes, Hedda, why don't you do that? *("Hedda Gabler" glares at them for a moment, then exits through the curtain.)*

HEDDA. DON'T GO BACK THERE! *(To Patrick and Steven.)* Can't I STOP her?

STEVEN. Sweetie, remember, it's only a play.

HEDDA. Right. *(Suddenly, wild music plays on a piano.)*

"GEORGE TESMAN." Darling! *(No response.)* Darling! Don't play that tonight! Not this of all nights!

HEDDA. *(Going to "George.")* Don't you KNOW her?

"GEORGE TESMAN." Oh please, think of Aunt Rina!

HEDDA. *(To all of the characters:)* Don't ANY of you KNOW her?

"GEORGE TESMAN." And poor Eilert! *(The music stops.)*

"HEDDA GABLER." *(Offstage.)* Of course! And think of Aunt Julie — and why not everyone else? I'm thinking about the whole lot of you, Tesman. I promise to shut up.

"GEORGE TESMAN." Oh, Mrs. Elvsted, how thoughtless to

work this way while Hedda's grieving so.

HEDDA. *(A plea.)* TESMAN! For God's sake, do something!

"GEORGE TESMAN." *(Lowering his voice.)* Why don't you take Aunt Julie's empty room? And I can drop by at night and we can work without disturbing a soul —

"HEDDA GABLER." *(Offstage.)* I hear you! I hear everything you're saying, Tesman! But what about me? What am I supposed to do at home all alone?

HEDDA. *(Softly.)* Exactly.

"GEORGE TESMAN." Well — the Judge will peek in every now and then, won't you Judge?

"JUDGE BRACK." With happiness. Every night. We'll get along just dandily.

"HEDDA GABLER." *(Offstage.)* Do you think so, Judge?

HEDDA. No!

"HEDDA GABLER." Really?

HEDDA. DON'T!

"HEDDA GABLER." Now that you're the big shot?

HEDDA. STOP! *(A loud gunshot. The real Hedda screams, loudly and wrenchingly. Her screams echo beyond what her voice can produce. She goes to the actor playing "George Tesman." Her hands reach for him, stopping just short of his face. He makes eye contact with her. The actors pause onstage. They pause for a long time. The actors playing Thea and the Judge glance at "George Tesman," who's forgotten his line.)*

"JUDGE BRACK." *(Prompting, softly.)* That Hedda …

"GEORGE TESMAN." That Hedda and her pistols! Darling, really! *(Slightly confused, he goes to the curtain and pulls it back. "Hedda Gabler" lies sprawled on a sofa in the room. There's a bullet-hole in her temple. "George Tesman" goes to her, and stops. He touches her head, and screams in horror.)* She shot herself! She shot herself in the head! Oh God, just imagine, oh … *(He collapses to the ground, holding her. A moment.)*

"JUDGE BRACK." My God. People don't do things like that. *(After a silent moment, the scene vanishes. Hedda sits, alone. A long moment. We hear a smattering of applause, which builds to a tremendous ovation. Hedda stands, breathing hard. Her breathing increases until she's gasping the air in large gulps, as the applause continues. It fades. She stands alone. Her breaths subside. Patrick and Steven go to her, and put their arms around her. They sit for a quiet moment. Hedda gathers herself, and turns to them.)*

HEDDA. So that is how it is.

PATRICK. If people could only see their own lives re-enacted onstage for the amusement of others — think of the therapy it would save.

HEDDA. But instead they get me.

STEVEN. Darling, that's not to be taken lightly. You're more than plenty for an evening out. *(Mammy enters, in her slave attire. She stops, and draws herself up with dignity. A moment.)*

MAMMY. You got de blues, Miss Hedda? *(Hedda nods.)* Now here's what we's gwynne do. We's gwynne go back home, and I fix you up a nice cuppa tea and putchu in a nice steamin' bath. Then I draws you a nice big fire, and you set by it 'til de mawnin'. An' if you fall asleep for awhiles, that's good. An' if you don't, den at least you gots yo Mammy lookin' after you. And come mawnin' time, mebbe things won't be no different, but at least we gots de mawnin'. *(Hedda nods. Patrick, Steven, and Hedda brush themselves off and stand.)* We's best be headin' on home. *(A moment. They walk offstage together, leaving it empty and dark. Lights fade.)*

End of Play

Here I Is

from "The Further Adventures of Hedda Gabler"

Score

Music & Lyrics: Jeff Whitty
Arr. Patrick Barnes

Cue: FEMALE VOICE: *"Oh, fiddle-dee-dee, Mammy, can't you hurry?"*
MAMMY: *"I says I's-"* (stinger)

Mammy

C7 F F sus4/B♭ Mammy: *a capella*

Mammy dialogue
Cue: *"I's telling you, I ain' goin'!"*

Hedda: *"And deep in my heart I believe we really must love, all of us, each other. For if we all try-really try to be happy, if we work, and we must work, if we work we will succeed someday. Some day we will find happiness, all of us, together."*

Here I

7
M

F F sus4/B♭
Rubato, colla voce

is Here I is_____ On de edge____ of some-thin' new.

Hedda: *"We must look to the future, the future generations, whose lives we shall never know."*

13
M

F F sus4/B♭

Down and out I's work-in' all de time I so tired____ of feel-in' blue.

18
M

B♭ F/A

Hedda: *"We'll turn from sadness and anger, and treat each other with diginity and, yes, love."*

But when I's cre-a-ted I din' get ed-u-ca-ted____ And it

23
M

Gm F B♭ *start a build*

look like my life gon' be long_____

Hedda: *"For though today may be awful, tomorrow-tomorrow is another day!"*

Who'd live for-ev-er____ at

28
M

F/A Gm C7 **In tempo, full gospel**

dis kin-na price? I jis' don' know what I done wrong. Here I is Here I

33
M

F sus4/B♭ F

is_____ I be sim - ple, so dey say____ I learn a word I ne-ver hear be-fore When dey

38
M

F sus4/B♭ B♭ *full build* F/A Gm

call____ me a "cli - ché" But dat gon' be chan-gin' Yeah! I's gwynne be chan-gin' No more feel-in' sad and for-

©2008

Here I Is

Here I Is

3

M: gone with the wind And I'll stand cen-ter and take a bow_____ I re-wrote my his-t'ry and I'm

Ch: ah - - - - - ah You take that bow, Ahh -

M: chang - ing my life And no - bo - dy can stop me now!_____

Ch: ah no - bo - dy can stop me now!_____

APPENDIX

ALTERNATIVE LINE (Page 34)

Suffering Jesus' "Those Romans do not mess around" may be replaced with "Mel Gibson does not mess around."

ACT TWO, SCENE 5 (Page 56)

Following is dialogue between Hedda and the Judge to be played in pantomime in Act Two, Scene 5:

"HEDDA GABLER." What did you just say about the pistol?
"JUDGE BRACK." That Eilert Lovborg must have stolen it.
"HEDDA GABLER." Stolen? Why?
"JUDGE BRACK." It's the only explanation I can think of.
"HEDDA GABLER." Of course.
"JUDGE BRACK." He'd been here just this morning, right?
"HEDDA GABLER." Yes.
"JUDGE BRACK." Think, Hedda. Did you ever leave him alone in the room?
"HEDDA GABLER." Perhaps — just for a minute. I went to the hall.
"JUDGE BRACK." And your pistol-case was where?
"HEDDA GABLER." Locked away —
"JUDGE BRACK." Oh really?
"HEDDA GABLER." It was on top of the desk.
"JUDGE BRACK." Have you checked to see where the pistols are now?
"HEDDA GABLER." No.
"JUDGE BRACK." Don't worry. I recognized the pistol that Eilert Lovborg had when they found him, dead. I saw it yesterday. Here.
"HEDDA GABLER." Do you have it?
"JUDGE BRACK." The police do.
"HEDDA GABLER." And they'll do what with it?
"JUDGE BRACK." Trace it to its owner. They will try.

"HEDDA GABLER." And will they find the owner?

"JUDGE BRACK." Not if I keep quiet.

"HEDDA GABLER." And if you don't?

"JUDGE BRACK." You could tell them it was stolen.

"HEDDA GABLER." I'd sooner die.

"JUDGE BRACK." People SAY things like that, but they don't DO them.

"HEDDA GABLER." And if the gun turns out not to be stolen, and they find its owner — what would happen?

"JUDGE BRACK." I imagine there'll be a tremendous scandal. Just what you're afraid of. You'd of course testify in court, right alongside Lovborg's friends in the underworld. And you'll have to answer the question of why you gave Lovborg the pistol in the first place. And what, Mrs. Tesman, will people assume then?

"HEDDA GABLER." I — I didn't think of it that way.

"JUDGE BRACK." But you're fine, my dear. As long as I keep my mouth shut.

An option for the "Play Within the Play" is to make it a conceptual production of *Hedda Gabler* — for example, a production set in the 1950s. The following lines may be used in this case:

PATRICK. Oh, but it's practically over.

HEDDA. Who are THEY?

STEVEN. This is YOUR PLAY, darling!

HEDDA. *(Recoiling.)* Oh, no, eck! *(Surveying the stage.)* Wait — this doesn't look anything like my life!

PATRICK. Welcome to the turbulent waters of the "concept production."

HEDDA. I don't get it.

PATRICK. Audiences rarely do.

STEVEN. Oh, it's not so bad. Feel lucky the play's not set underwater or in a concentration camp or something.

HEDDA. Well, which one's which?

(Dialogue continues with Steven's, "Well, that's Thea Elvsted ... ")

SUGGESTED CHARACTER BREAKDOWN

ACTOR ONE — Hedda Gabler

ACTOR TWO — Mammy, Shamari Robinson

ACTOR THREE — Tesman, First Male Voice, "Judge Brack"

ACTOR FOUR — Medea, Cassandra, Lotion Lady, Little Orphan Annie, Dorothy Gale, Dying Woman, "Hedda Gabler"

ACTOR FIVE — Flossie, Tosca, Woman in Pink, Masha, Diane Johnson, Black Jesus, Dying Junkie, "Thea Elvsted" (could also play Little Orphan Annie/Dorothy Gale)

ACTOR SIX — Patrick, Jar-Jar Binks, Suffering Jesus

ACTOR SEVEN — Steven, Musical Jesus

ACTOR EIGHT — Eilert Lovborg, Second Male Voice, Judge Brack, Jesus the Carpenter, Chainsaw Killer, "George Tesman"

PROPERTY LIST

Pistol
Book
Bottle of Shout
Tea and scones
Body dropping from overhead
Laundry, washboard
Winged chariot
Steamer trunks
Cell phone
Bottle of lotion
Sign with arrow
Chainsaw, hockey mask
Large purse-like bag with blood-stained dress
Cocktails
Baby
Icarus falling from sky
Cocktail shaker
Cigarette
Marijuana joint
Soda gun with hose
Gun
Curtain
Feathered hat
Papers

SOUND EFFECTS

Wild music on piano
Gunshots
Clapping
Curtain being pulled back
Operatic soprano trill
Chainsaw
Screams of the dying
Apocalyptic sound, echoing and burning
Bird chirping
Musical refrain

NEW PLAYS

★ **GUARDIANS by Peter Morris.** In this unflinching look at war, a disgraced American soldier discloses the truth about Abu Ghraib prison, and a clever English journalist reveals how he faked a similar story for the London tabloids. "Compelling, sympathetic and powerful." *–NY Times.* "Sends you into a state of moral turbulence." *–Sunday Times (UK).* "Nothing short of remarkable." *–Village Voice.* [1M, 1W] ISBN: 978-0-8222-2177-7

★ **BLUE DOOR by Tanya Barfield.** Three generations of men (all played by one actor), from slavery through Black Power, challenge Lewis, a tenured professor of mathematics, to embark on a journey combining past and present. "A teasing flare for words." *–Village Voice.* "Unfailingly thought-provoking." *–LA Times.* "The play moves with the speed and logic of a dream." *–Seattle Weekly.* [2M] ISBN: 978-0-8222-2209-5

★ **THE INTELLIGENT DESIGN OF JENNY CHOW by Rolin Jones.** This irreverent "techno-comedy" chronicles one brilliant woman's quest to determine her heritage and face her fears with the help of her astounding creation called Jenny Chow. "Boldly imagined." *–NY Times.* "Fantastical and funny." *–Variety.* "Harvests many laughs and finally a few tears." *–LA Times.* [3M, 3W] ISBN: 978-0-8222-2071-8

★ **SOUVENIR by Stephen Temperley.** Florence Foster Jenkins, a wealthy society eccentric, suffers under the delusion that she is a great coloratura soprano—when in fact the opposite is true. "Hilarious and deeply touching. Incredibly moving and breathtaking." *–NY Daily News.* "A sweet love letter of a play." *–NY Times.* "Wildly funny. Completely charming." *–Star-Ledger.* [1M, 1W] ISBN: 978-0-8222-2157-9

★ **ICE GLEN by Joan Ackermann.** In this touching period comedy, a beautiful poetess dwells in idyllic obscurity on a Berkshire estate with a band of unlikely cohorts. "A beautifully written story of nature and change." *–Talkin' Broadway.* "A lovely play which will leave you with a lot to think about." *–CurtainUp.* "Funny, moving and witty." *–Metroland (Boston).* [4M, 3W] ISBN: 978-0-8222-2175-3

★ **THE LAST DAYS OF JUDAS ISCARIOT by Stephen Adly Guirgis.** Set in a time-bending, darkly comic world between heaven and hell, this play reexamines the plight and fate of the New Testament's most infamous sinner. "An unforced eloquence that finds the poetry in lowdown street talk." *–NY Times.* "A real jaw-dropper." *–Variety.* "An extraordinary play." *–Guardian (UK).* [10M, 5W] ISBN: 978-0-8222-2082-4

DRAMATISTS PLAY SERVICE, INC.
440 Park Avenue South, New York, NY 10016 212-683-8960 Fax 212-213-1539
postmaster@dramatists.com www.dramatists.com

NEW PLAYS

★ **THE GREAT AMERICAN TRAILER PARK MUSICAL music and lyrics by David Nehls, book by Betsy Kelso.** Pippi, a stripper on the run, has just moved into Armadillo Acres, wreaking havoc among the tenants of Florida's most exclusive trailer park. "Adultery, strippers, murderous ex-boyfriends, Costco and the Ice Capades. Undeniable fun." *–NY Post.* "Joyful and un-ashamedly vulgar." *–The New Yorker.* "Sparkles with treasure." *–New York Sun.* [2M, 5W] ISBN: 978-0-8222-2137-1

★ **MATCH by Stephen Belber.** When a young Seattle couple meet a prominent New York choreographer, they are led on a fraught journey that will change their lives forever. "Uproariously funny, deeply moving, enthralling theatre." *–NY Daily News.* "Prolific laughs and ear-to-ear smiles." *–NY Magazine.* [2M, 1W] ISBN: 978-0-8222-2020-6

★ **MR. MARMALADE by Noah Haidle.** Four-year-old Lucy's imaginary friend, Mr. Marmalade, doesn't have much time for her—not to mention he has a cocaine addiction and a penchant for pornography. "Alternately hilarious and heartbreaking." *–The New Yorker.* "A mature and accomplished play." *–LA Times.* "Scathingly observant comedy." *–Miami Herald.* [4M, 2W] ISBN: 978-0-8222-2142-5

★ **MOONLIGHT AND MAGNOLIAS by Ron Hutchinson.** Three men cloister themselves as they work tirelessly to reshape a screenplay that's just not working—*Gone with the Wind.* "Consumers of vintage Hollywood insider stories will eat up Hutchinson's diverting conjecture." *–Variety.* "A lot of fun." *–NY Post.* "A Hollywood dream-factory farce." *–Chicago Sun-Times.* [3M, 1W] ISBN: 978-0-8222-2084-8

★ **THE LEARNED LADIES OF PARK AVENUE by David Grimm, translated and freely adapted from Molière's Les Femmes Savantes.** Dicky wants to marry Betty, but her mother's plan is for Betty to wed a most pompous man. "A brave, brainy and barmy revision." *–Hartford Courant.* "A rare but welcome bird in contemporary theatre." *–New Haven Register.* "Roll over Cole Porter." *–Boston Globe.* [5M, 5W] ISBN: 978-0-8222-2135-7

★ **REGRETS ONLY by Paul Rudnick.** A sparkling comedy of Manhattan manners that explores the latest topics in marriage, friendships and squandered riches. "One of the funniest quip-meisters on the planet." *–NY Times.* "Precious moments of hilarity. Devastatingly accurate political and social satire." *–BackStage.* "Great fun." *–CurtainUp.* [3M, 3W] ISBN: 978-0-8222-2223-1

DRAMATISTS PLAY SERVICE, INC.
440 Park Avenue South, New York, NY 10016 212-683-8960 Fax 212-213-1539
postmaster@dramatists.com www.dramatists.com

NEW PLAYS

★ **AFTER ASHLEY by Gina Gionfriddo.** A teenager is unwillingly thrust into the national spotlight when a family tragedy becomes talk-show fodder. "A work that virtually any audience would find accessible." *–NY Times.* "Deft characterization and caustic humor." *–NY Sun.* "A smart satirical drama." *–Variety.* [4M, 2W] ISBN: 978-0-8222-2099-2

★ **THE RUBY SUNRISE by Rinne Groff.** Twenty-five years after Ruby struggles to realize her dream of inventing the first television, her daughter faces similar battles of faith as she works to get Ruby's story told on network TV. "Measured and intelligent, optimistic yet clear-eyed." *–NY Magazine.* "Maintains an exciting sense of ingenuity." *–Village Voice.* "Sinuous theatrical flair." *–Broadway.com.* [3M, 4W] ISBN: 978-0-8222-2140-1

★ **MY NAME IS RACHEL CORRIE taken from the writings of Rachel Corrie, edited by Alan Rickman and Katharine Viner.** This solo piece tells the story of Rachel Corrie who was killed in Gaza by an Israeli bulldozer set to demolish a Palestinian home. "Heartbreaking urgency. An invigoratingly detailed portrait of a passionate idealist." *–NY Times.* "Deeply authentically human." *–USA Today.* "A stunning dramatization." *–CurtainUp.* [1W] ISBN: 978-0-8222-2222-4

★ **ALMOST, MAINE by John Cariani.** This charming midwinter night's dream of a play turns romantic clichés on their ear as it chronicles the painfully hilarious amorous adventures (and misadventures) of residents of a remote northern town that doesn't quite exist. "A whimsical approach to the joys and perils of romance." *–NY Times.* "Sweet, poignant and witty." *–NY Daily News.* "Aims for the heart by way of the funny bone." *–Star-Ledger.* [2M, 2W] ISBN: 978-0-8222-2156-2

★ **Mitch Albom's TUESDAYS WITH MORRIE by Jeffrey Hatcher and Mitch Albom, based on the book by Mitch Albom.** The true story of Brandeis University professor Morrie Schwartz and his relationship with his student Mitch Albom. "A touching, life-affirming, deeply emotional drama." *–NY Daily News.* "You'll laugh. You'll cry." *–Variety.* "Moving and powerful." *–NY Post.* [2M] ISBN: 978-0-8222-2188-3

★ **DOG SEES GOD: CONFESSIONS OF A TEENAGE BLOCKHEAD by Bert V. Royal.** An abused pianist and a pyromaniac ex-girlfriend contribute to the teen-angst of America's most hapless kid. "A welcome antidote to the notion that the *Peanuts* gang provides merely American cuteness." *–NY Times.* "Hysterically funny." *–NY Post.* "The *Peanuts* kids have finally come out of their shells." *–Time Out.* [4M, 4W] ISBN: 978-0-8222-2152-4

DRAMATISTS PLAY SERVICE, INC.
440 Park Avenue South, New York, NY 10016 212-683-8960 Fax 212-213-1539
postmaster@dramatists.com   www.dramatists.com

NEW PLAYS

★ **RABBIT HOLE by David Lindsay-Abaire.** Winner of the 2007 Pulitzer Prize. Becca and Howie Corbett have everything a couple could want until a life-shattering accident turns their world upside down. "An intensely emotional examination of grief, laced with wit." *–Variety.* "A transcendent and deeply affecting new play." *–Entertainment Weekly.* "Painstakingly beautiful." *–BackStage.* [2M, 3W] ISBN: 978-0-8222-2154-8

★ **DOUBT, A Parable by John Patrick Shanley.** Winner of the 2005 Pulitzer Prize and Tony Award. Sister Aloysius, a Bronx school principal, takes matters into her own hands when she suspects the young Father Flynn of improper relations with one of the male students. "All the elements come invigoratingly together like clockwork." *–Variety.* "Passionate, exquisite, important, engrossing." *–NY Newsday.* [1M, 3W] ISBN: 978-0-8222-2219-4

★ **THE PILLOWMAN by Martin McDonagh.** In an unnamed totalitarian state, an author of horrific children's stories discovers that someone has been making his stories come true. "A blindingly bright black comedy." *–NY Times.* "McDonagh's least forgiving, bravest play." *–Variety.* "Thoroughly startling and genuinely intimidating." *–Chicago Tribune.* [4M, 5 bit parts (2M, 1W, 1 boy, 1 girl)] ISBN: 978-0-8222-2100-5

★ **GREY GARDENS book by Doug Wright, music by Scott Frankel, lyrics by Michael Korie.** The hilarious and heartbreaking story of Big Edie and Little Edie Bouvier Beale, the eccentric aunt and cousin of Jacqueline Kennedy Onassis, once bright names on the social register who became East Hampton's most notorious recluses. "An experience no passionate theatergoer should miss." *–NY Times.* "A unique and unmissable musical." *–Rolling Stone.* [4M, 3W, 2 girls] ISBN: 978-0-8222-2181-4

★ **THE LITTLE DOG LAUGHED by Douglas Carter Beane.** Mitchell Green could make it big as the hot new leading man in Hollywood if Diane, his agent, could just keep him in the closet. "Devastatingly funny." *–NY Times.* "An out-and-out delight." *–NY Daily News.* "Full of wit and wisdom." *–NY Post.* [2M, 2W] ISBN: 978-0-8222-2226-2

★ **SHINING CITY by Conor McPherson.** A guilt-ridden man reaches out to a therapist after seeing the ghost of his recently deceased wife. "Haunting, inspired and glorious." *–NY Times.* "Simply breathtaking and astonishing." *–Time Out.* "A thoughtful, artful, absorbing new drama." *–Star-Ledger.* [3M, 1W] ISBN: 978-0-8222-2187-6

DRAMATISTS PLAY SERVICE, INC.
440 Park Avenue South, New York, NY 10016   212-683-8960   Fax 212-213-1539
postmaster@dramatists.com   www.dramatists.com